RHINESTONE Jewelry

FIGURALS, ANIMALS, and WHIMSICALS

Identification & Values
Marcia "Sparkles" Brown

COLLECTOR BOOKS
A Division of Schroeder Publishing Co., Inc.

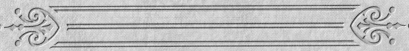

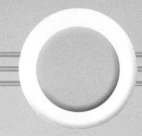

Front cover:
1. Cat fur clip, sterling silver. The blue-glass, scalloped edges form the body. $95.00
2. Lovebird heart – two loving parents feed their young hatchling. Made in France, $265.00
3. Interlaced rust and green cabochon form turtle shell. $40.00
4. Emerald green, faceted rhinestone-body insect. $65.00
5. Praying mantis, 1930s, enameled white metal. $135.00
6. *Capri* dancing bird. $85.00
7. Red and clear rhinestone fish from the 1930s. $195.00
8. Jack and Jill water carriers are fur clips. $95.00
9. *Kirks Folly* lyre-playing angel. $48.00.

Back cover:
1. Italian hand-blown glass necklace – doves with holly leaves and berries. $145.00
2. Lucite and enamel cow still has charm after 50 years. $185.00
3. Silken blue birds painted on metal. $95.00
4. *Valentino* Mediterranean Sea shell bracelet. Made in Italy. $215.00
5. Hopalong Cassidy mounted on his horse at the Bar XX Ranch. $85.00
6. Connestoga covered wagon with oxen. $45.00
7. Hopalong's gun breaks away to reveal his name on the inside of the metal brooch. $68.00

Cover design by Beth Summers
Book design by Christen Byrd
Cover photography by Charles R. Lynch

COLLECTOR BOOKS
P.O. Box 3009
Paducah, Kentucky 42002-3009
www.collectorbooks.com

Copyright © 2006 Marcia Brown

The current values in this book should be used only as a guide. They are not intended to set prices, which vary from one section of the country to another. Auction prices as well as dealer prices vary greatly and are affected by condition as well as demand. Neither the author nor the publisher assumes responsibility for any losses that might be incurred as a result of consulting this guide.

Searching for a Publisher?

We are always looking for people knowledgeable within their fields. If you feel that there is a real need for a book on your collectible subject and have a large comprehensive collection, contact Collector Books.

Proudly printed and bound in the
United States of America

Contents

Dedication

This fifth book on the American art form of costume jewelry could not, and would not, exist without Kenneth Arthur Brown. He is the founder of the private Brown Rhinestone Museum. His encouragement and support has led me down a path that I could not have taken alone.

He patiently has spent weeks, months, and years on shopping trips, repairing my jewelry, and learning photography to help create these books.

Many of our readers have written to praise the wonderful pictures in the books. They are the dedicated work of this man… my husband of 56 years.

Introduction

Unsigned Beauties of Costume Jewelry and *Signed Beauties of Costume Jewelry Volumes I & II* concentrated on the beauty of costume jewelry. By learning all you could about how the jewelry is created, you cultivated your appreciation of the American art form of rhinestone jewelry.

This book is dedicated to the little child that lies forever within us.
Turning the pages will help you relive the days of your youth.

As you look at these critters and whimsicals, your mouth will start turning up at the edges, the light in your eyes will soften, your blood pressure will start dropping, and a smile will brighten your face.

Memories will come pouring into your daydreams of sunlit meadows filled with flowers that attracted the butterflies. Perhaps the family dog or purring cat you had will come into view.

Remember the woodsy smell of the forest, the pungent smell of the barnyard. The calls of the birds in the trees still echo in your mind; the bounty of the ocean and beaches of our wonderful world that you enjoyed when you were young still linger in your memory, just waiting for you to recollect them.

Come, let me treat you and take you back to those golden times.

Collecting

General Rules

There are rules of the game in all that is attempted. Learning these rules can save a lot of wasted time and money whether it be in the stock market, video games, antique furniture buying, or collecting rhinestone jewelry. A well prepared, studied approach can enlarge the enjoyment of the hunt.

• Know what is being sold today, to know what was sold in the yesteryear. Visit retail outlets, ask to look at today's modern jewelry. Caress the jewelry, let your fingers walk all over the front and back, weigh the piece in your hands. Make a thorough study of the finishes, and the fittings used. There are many "antique" items being manufactured today. A very good source to keep up to date on copied old items being produced (complete with fake factory and the original company marks) is "Repronews.com" on the internet.

If the original company is reintroducing a former jewelry piece, it should be noted. For instance, Trifari manufactured a new jelly-belly rooster but carefully noted the year of production. Another jewelry company, Tortolani, has been revived by the family and today's production has a burr, or pimple, following the name on the back side.

Plan your schedule to allow you to visit antique shows, jewelry dealers, collectors, and yard sales. Take the time to ask questions as you use your hands and fingers to note the difference in the jewelry of yesterday and today's productions.

Begin a notebook and make entries. Compare information that has been obtained as a method of checking and double-checking your resources to sift out misinformation. Don't trust your memory to keep the file. If you write it down in a small notebook, it can travel with you.

• Do your research homework to buy with confidence. Catalogs and computers have thousands of pictures and prices for your at-home research. Familiarize yourself with jewelry terms and learn the definition of the words to enable you to understand a written description.

• Study history date lines to help establish age. When a piece is said to be 100 years old from Czechoslovakia you know that isn't true because your study of history tells you that it wasn't a country until 1917.

The copyright, an encircled C, denotes that the design was registered with the Patent Office after 1954. Aurora borealis rhinestones were first used in rhinestone jewelry after 1953. The gun-metal finish was only produced in American jewelry from 1953 to 1955.

This information, and much more, can be obtained by reviewing recent books written by experts. Visit your local library to check out jewelry books to see if you wish to extend your own library. When you are ready to build your own library, check the used book sections for bargains.

• Remember, age is no guarantee of value. John Humphries, noted radio and television personality, always shows his 200-year-old scarab ring as proof of this rule. Despite its antiquity, it is valued at $200.00 — this figures out to a dollar a year.

It is nice to know the approximate age of a piece, but condition, condition, condition is the most important factor in pricing.

• Learn the various conditions used to price the item. The patina of age is beautiful, and the softening of color can be expected. Whether the jewelry has been well taken care of, or handled roughly will establish the price almost like coin values. Rankings of poor, fair, good, and mint can be applied to all antiques.

A repainted pedal car does not lose value, but a newly-painted pot-metal brooch can loose over 50% of its value. A pendant without the original chain will be worth only about 60% of an authentic chain and pendant.

• Carry a magnifying loupe and measuring tape when you are shopping. Bursting with pride of the wonderful bargain I had just picked up, I showed it to my husband. "That's nice", he said, "but how do you pin it on?" Taking out the loupe I had left a home, I turned the lovely brooch over and, to my horror, found that all the fastener parts had been filed off! Yes, I had bought a piece of costume jewelry that was intended to be part of a Christmas tree mounted on black velvet and framed.

Please learn from my example. Ask to take the piece to better light, or even out in the sunlight to thoroughly examine the back very carefully to detect soldering repairs or pin back replacements.

• If matching pieces to complete a set or parure, have the actual item along (or a picture) to allow you a visual comparison to confirm the match. The same company could have produced a variety of finishes from the same model and used a variety of stones to complete the jewelry. Always match silver plate to silver plate, gold plate to gold plate. Even check to be sure that the types and colors of the rhinestones follow the same designs.

If you have been hunting for a rare shape or color stone that you need, it is very important that you have done a good job matching to complete returning the jewelry to its original condition.

• Thoroughly examine the item at all angles before buying. If the jewelry is supposedly in the original box, make sure that the box was made to accommodate each piece of the set.

If that piece marked "Eisenberg Originals" has Phillips screws used to put the layers together you are looking at a copy, BEWARE. If the dealer has multiples of a "rare" item, ask yourself how it could be rare if it is so readily available.

• Don't be shy about asking questions. If they have the time, most people like to share their knowledge. At a garage sale, the family legends can help you to determine the age by using the 30 year factor for each generation that has owned the item. If they say the piece was their grandmothers, you would figure 3 generations times 30 and arrive at an approximate age of 90 years, establishing the 1910 decade.

The stories of how the item came into the family's possession are priceless, even if they are sometimes far fetched. The well-dress elderly lady who brought a brooch to show me that her friends had bought as a souvenir on their honeymoon at Florence, Italy told the story well and had the proof because the piece was marked "Florenza" (an American company). Despite my tactful correction, she left with the brooch and story still intact.

• See if it is possible to have an expert give you some guidance. Check community calendars and see if courses are being offered at the community college or local university. Ask your Chamber of Commerce if there are any costume jewelry or antique clubs nearby. See if there is a local appraiser that would offer you some private lessons.

I found out about the Vintage Fashion and Costume Jewelry Club, an international organization, that has four publications a year, from a friendly dealer.

The Maloney Resource Directory has a section devoted to jewelry, with complete addresses (both snail and email) for contacting experts. Your local library should have a reference copy for your use.

• Buy what you like, it may become your family's heirloom. But first, examine the piece thoroughly to check the condition. Ask yourself what caught your attention: "Why do you want to own it? ", "What will you do with it?", "Is the price right?"

One of the most important questions will be, "Will I ever see another one like this?" Also ask yourself, "Would I ever want to sell it?" and, "If so, could I make a profit?"

• Check condition before buying, repair or restoration usually lowers the value. Become a triage nurse and evaluate the patient's injuries. Plating worn off down to the base metal or a soldering job needed are clear work for an expert in restoration. It can be costly for you, and the possibility of affecting the value of the jewelry should be thoroughly considered.

If the necklace needs to be restrung, remember it isn't just putting back one or two beads. Each strand will need to be done, and all pieces will have to be there to insure that each strand will drape properly. Double-knotted beads will cost more to restore.

A simple repair job would be the replacement of missing stones. Ornate, large, or unusually-colored stones may be hard to find. Do you have a supply of loose stones or damaged pieces to salvage the stone? If not, will you have to pay to have the work done? A link that needs to be closed, or a jump ring that needs to be replaced would fall into the repair category.

• When buying, ask for a written sales slip with qualifying statements about the jewelry. The slip should contain: the seller's name, address, and/or business phone number; a complete description of your purchase (including the maker or source); approximate age and condition (with specific reference to repairs or restoration); quantity of items; any special terms of the purchase; purchase price; and date of sale.

Verbal statements and agreements can led to misunderstanding. The sales slip will confirm all the conditions of the transaction.

• Buy from reputable dealers. In a friendly chat, check out their references just as you would the appliance store. How long they have been in the business assures you that they are not fly-by-nights. Ask yourself, "Were they willing to answer my inquires and let me handle and closely examine the item?"

• Check out refund and return policies. When buying, the seller has the right to ask the dealer for a written sales slip with qualifying statements. Will they accept returns? If so, do they give credit or will they refund? How good is their guarantee? A reputable dealer will be glad to answer the questions of a careful buyer.

If you have carefully thought it through, checked your budget, and you like it, BUY IT!! Once you have passed up a piece, the odds that you will have the opportunity to purchase it at a later date are highly improbable.

Now you have bought that treasure and taken it to your abode. Don't bury it in the chest of drawers, wrap it up in tissue paper, or put it in a plastic bag. Keep the original box if it bears the store or jewelry's name. Don't tear the little metal tag off of the necklace, it is a trademark symbol of the manufacturer.

The following rules can be applied to the care and storage of almost any antique or collectible. You have your investment to protect.

• Never store a treasure in the attic or basement. Dampness and heat are the enemies of all antiques and collectibles. Mold can develop in the basement. Heat and sunlight can rot fabrics and papers. Your treasures will be left undefended, exposed to mice, bugs, insects, and all sorts of crawly things.

• Protect item from extreme temperatures. Glued-in stones have been known to fall out of the settings as the aged glue reacts to temperature changes. Hiding the jewelry in the freezer can cause the stones to crack.

• Protect item from sunlight. Sun can fade enamel, and cause a deterioration of necklace stringing materials. Even glass beads can crystallize, crack, and chip.

• Research cleaning methods, using only tried and true methods. Test any new method on an old or already damaged piece to check the results. Never attempt a repair job before dusting that piece of jewelry to see if it is just on the surface. You do not want to disturb the piece unless really necessary.

• Never use a cleaning product or method that was not in use when your treasure was new. It is recommended that you never, never immerse rhinestone in liquid that can seep in between the glass and the foil backing.

On silver, paste silver polish will leave white residue in cracks. Those blacked areas on silver accent the dimensions and design. A special oxidation process was used to achieve this beautiful finish. Polishing will make that beautiful old piece look like something new from the store…do you really want that look? Just use a rouge cloth and gently rub the jewelry to remove excess surface soiling.

• When in doubt on cleaning or restoring, DON'T. At least take some time to think it over. Once you convert clip earrings to pierced you have reduced the value of that set over 20%. If the necklace is too short, do not alter the chain. Make your own necklace extensions by using a piece of chain with a jump ring on one end and a large ring on the other. Then fasten the jump ring around the end of necklace, and hook the original fastener in the next extension. Check to make sure it is secure and you are ready to go out in front of your admiring public.

• Develop a method of inventory. It will help you to know what you paid for the item when considering whether to part with or sell the piece. The inventory should at least denote the amount you spent, a brief description of the item, and how many matching pieces there were.

• Keep sales slip where it can be found. The original sales slip on a Christian Dior brooch bought in Paris, France was still attached. The slip identified the year, the Grosse of Germany company that manufactured it, and the number of francs that were spent on it. This almost doubled the antique asking price.

• Make sure that information and documentation is left to help your heirs. Without a guide, they will have no idea of the value of your jewelry. It will make a difference on how they will handle it… heirloom, sold for a premium, yard sale, or donations. And the insurance company will need the information if there is a claim. A note of caution, most companies will require a rider on your home owner's policy if the jewelry is valued at over $2,500.

Doing What Comes Naturally

Where does one start a collection? At the beginning, I suppose. You start by picking up that little bit of color that your blouse or jacket needs to complete your outfit. Or perhaps you inherited your mother's jewelry box. Cat, dog, or horse lovers seem to have friends and relatives that find a gift of animal jewelry is appropriate. Soon you have a collection.

Horse jewelry was a fad in the 1940s, as were butterflies. Every well-dressed woman had to wear one and soon every jewelry box was filled with them.
The separation of the family during World War II led to the influx of hearts. Gifts from one loved one to another became the start of the sweetheart jewelry. To this very day, these pieces are highly collectible.

Jingle, jangle, here comes the advent of the charm bracelet in the 1950s. Each symbol dangling from the chain had special meaning. Sterling silver charms that had moveable parts were the epitome of style and the delight of many a teenage girl. Toasters with slices of bread that popped up, scissors that opened and shut, vehicles with wheels that moved, any item that was mechanical was prized.

In the 1960s, ballerinas danced their way into the heart of fashion. The tutu and the pirouette were used by most of the leading designers such as Trifari, Boucher, and Coro.

The years from 1940 to 1970 were the heyday years for the costume jewelry industry. Every hour of the work day, thousands of pieces poured out of the Rhode Island manufacturing plants.

This large volume created a legacy of jewelry for collectors. The sheer number of pieces for sale helped to keep the jewelry affordable. Since prices were so reasonable, it was easy to net colorful butterflies, be won over by a heart, or even perpetuate the dance with a ballerina.

With each piece purchased, the buyer increases their knowledge about this art form. Carrying out the style of Art Nouveau, the curve of the neck and chin on a cupid will soften your heart and beg to be adopted. Designers incorporated Art Deco's geometric forms and made stunning, shinning examples of the true American art form, rhinestone jewelry.

As you examine the piece, you might even catch a name inscribed on the back of the brooch. You have bought a signed piece and just realized that the name can be researched to learn more about the company. Now that your appetite has been whetted, you surely will want to find out if other companies made figurals. Did all companies offer them? The answer can be a challenge for a collector to prove.

Will the name on the back of a piece increase its value? That will depend on the quality and quantity produced by each company. In studying, you will learn that there are preferred companies that bring top dollar. A signature like Miriam Haskell, Boucher, or Joseff of Hollywood will be highly valued.

Many people start collections of signed beauties. Remember that there were over 1,000 jewelry companies based in the Providence, Rhode Island, area in the 1960s. How long do you suppose it would take to find every one? I have been collecting for almost 25 years; my count of companies has now reached 449.

After acquiring pieces that you like, you might be interested in why the designer/artist chose that particular object to be incorporated in his jewelry.

Many motifs have symbolic meaning:
 Anchors — hope and steadiness. Some believe it dates back to St. Clements who was roped to an anchor and tossed into the sea. By using the red, white, and blue rhinestones on the anchor, the patriotic touch is given to the ray of hope.
 Angels — messengers of God. They are often decorated with a holiday theme. The Florenza company made their cherub a Valentine's Day messenger, carrying a heart-shaped glass stone to a loved one.
 Animals — based upon their personality:
  Cats — playful, lazy, or hunters.
  Dogs — man's best friend, true to their masters.
  Foxes — smart and cunning.
  Horses — the sun. Dating back to the legend of the melting of the winged horse as the chariot was flown too close to the sun.
  Leopards, lions, and tigers — strength. The magnificence of a free animal.
  Pigs — good luck.
 Arrows — weapons of love and war. Cupid is armed with a bow to shoot the winged arrows of love. The archer will use his bow to shoot arrows at a target.

Birds—freedom of flight:
> *Blackbirds*—darkness of evil.
> *Cranes*—loyal and watchful.
> *Doves*—purity and peace. They are often depicted carrying an olive branch in their mouths.
> *Eagles*—liberty. The national bird of the United States of America.
> *Owls*—wisdom. Do you suppose that is because they can see every thing around them? See all, know all?
> *Peacocks*—vanity. They proudly spread and fan their tail feathers for all to enjoy.
> *Sparrows*—poor, common creatures.
> *Swallows*—spring's rebirth.

Butterflies—all the joys of summertime. The return of the flowers and the new animals.

Dragons—days of old. The legends of gallantry and chivalry among the knights.

Fish— the bounty of Earth. The ocean's offering to man.

Frogs—fertility. Remember "Froggy went a courting," an old nursery rhyme?

Hands—loving and kind. Folded in prayer or open in victory. Many hands are designed with feminine characteristics and holding such items as flowers and fans.

Hearts—ardor. Overflowing love.

Insects:
> *Ant*—industrious.
> *Bee*—hard worker.
> *Dragonfly*—summer.
> *Grasshopper*—lazy, fiddling around.
> *Scarab*—everlasting good luck.
> *Spider*—good luck.

Ivy—finding true love. A French legend that a girl should have ivy leaves near her heart to find a husband. Schiaprelli frequently used ivy leaves in her jewelry, perhaps perpetuating the legend.

Lizards—good eyesight. Most designs show the full length of the creature bedecked in dazzling rhinestones.

Moon and Stars:
> *Moon*—Chinese god of marriage.
> *Stars*—heaven.

People—power or homelands. They can resemble powerful, historical figures, ethnic groups, or represent countries.

Snakes—long life.

A collection of figurals, animals, and whimsicals is truly a study of jewelry, history, and legend.

Figurals

PEOPLE

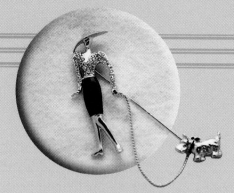

Carol Lee. This fashionable lady takes her dog for a stroll. $74.00

A gust of wind catches a lady walking her dog. $95.00

Coro pins.
Chatelaine lady with dog. $75.00
Wind-blown lady with umbrella. $94.00
High-class lady and wolfhound chatelaine. $125.00

HAR hobo decked out in rhinestone. $68.00

HAR, three gentlemen of the road. $78.00

Rhinestone boy and dog chatelaine. $78.00

Sterling silver strollers, decked out in pearls
and rhinestones. $54.00 (each)

Danecraft sterling silver lady. $98.00

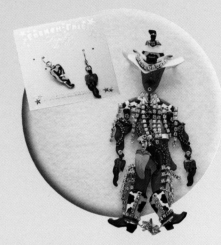

Lunch At The Ritz, "Chili Pepper Pete." Red
pepper guns and earrings. $205.00 (set)

JJ school kids.
Pearl faces and rhinestone accents.
$48.00 (each)

All Dolled Up, vintage buttons and beads.
Note buttonholes are positioned to
become the eyes. $48.00

All Dolled Up.
White and yellow beads form the body of this pin.
The face is hand painted and topped with a
black plastic hat. $48.00

This wooden Raggedy Ann is hand
carved and hand painted. $64.00

Blue plastic Indian and pony. $85.00

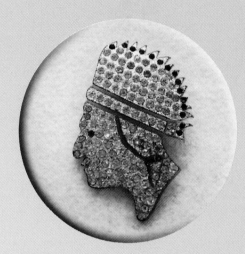

Indian head on Lucite back. $78.00

Parasol lady in rhinestone-studded
filigree skirt. $85.00
Dapper beau presents rhinestone
bouquet. $65.00

Rhinestone-faced lady holds on to
her hat and skirt. $78.00

Roaring 20s beauty.
Hand-crafted resin. $44.00

Colorful flapper beauty. $60.00

Delicate blonde beauty.
Pearl and feather accents.
$53.00

Bonetto sophisticated lady.
Watch pin with faceted stones.
$85.00

Vogue royal blackamoor page.
Sterling, pearl accent on staff.
$185.00

Ora brooch slide.
Shriner in full parade costume.
$165.00

Flower vendor's stall. $145.00

Organ grinder and his monkey. $70.00

Somehow I think this looks like a
bow-tied Frank Sinatra. $68.00

Gloucester fisherman. $68.00

Pioneer lady spins a fine chain. $110.00

This waiter has channel-set legs and
rhinestone-link feet. $60.00

"Sunbonnet Sue"
with watering can, sterling. $72.00

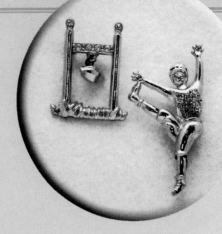

Scatter pins.
Goal post, and football kicker.
$48.00 (pair)

Plastic water skier. $85.00

Polcini diamanté golfer.
Resplendent in knickers. $64.00

Tortolani sport figures.
Golfer, baseball player, and bowler.
$55.00 – 68.00 (each)

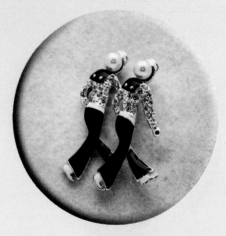

Wendy Gill.
Sailors on the town. $110.00

Plastic sailor in bright red.
$95.00

Nautical threesome.
Sailor with fish. $30.00
Bell-bottomed sailor with anchor. $95.00
Ship's steering wheel. $18.00

Signalman using his flags. $42.00
Saluting sailors in multicolored glass
stones. $65.00 (each)

Buddie from 1940s has painted cap. $98.00

1940s soldier with leather cap.
Hand-painted resin. $145.00

1940s blue-collared sailor.
Mounted on yellow anchor,
face is hand painted. $95.00

Graceful hand adorned with jewels. $35.00
Dainty hand holding a fan. $22.00

Brown hand holds a sunflower. $44.00
Hand holds a spray of pearl flowers. $28.00
Pair of hands hold a pearl. $22.00

Hand pins.
Hand holds rosey fan. $35.00
Red findertips adorn long white fingers. $45.00
Large blue stone adorns this golden hand. $34.00
Delicate rhinestone cuff decorates this silver
hand. $25.00

Celluloid girl with umbrella and flowerpot. $65.00
Three green-skirted hula girls. $45.00
Girl skier in bright red hat, scarf, and mittens. $34.00

DANCERS AND MUSICIANS

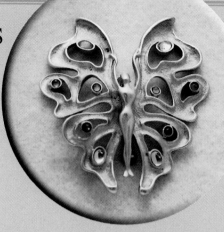

JJ dancer floats like a butterfly. $80.00

B. Schiffey 1986 male swinger pin.
Flat back, crackle glass stones. $98.00

Hobé hula dancer with pink flower in
her hair. $125.00

Napier sterling parure.
Four ballerina links in bracelet.
Brooch and earrings are individual dancers. $285.00

Coro male dancer has green cabochon face. $35.00
Corocraft Female dancer in red, white, and blue
rhinestones. $205.00

Trifari pearl-faced dancers.
Female has pavé bodice and rhinestones
dot her skirt and shoes.
Male has pavé vest and rhinestones dot his
tights and boots. $290.00 (pair)

CoroCraft sterling pin.
Model of famous Parisian dancer
Josephine Baker. $400.00

Trifari scarecrows with Peking glass heads.
Female has full skirt and pavé bodice. $85.00
Males have rhinestone scarves. $200.00 (pair)

Trifari ballerinas.
Pavé bodice, diamanté ruffle. $140.00
Green rhinestones on tutu and crown. $195.00

Sterling silver chatelaine.
Musical note and ballet couple. $78.00

Sterling vermeil ballet dancers.
White glass stone accents. $85.00

Ballet dancer with pear-shaped topaz body. $75.00
Nolan Miller dancer with diamanté stones. $145.00

Norma Jean brooch.
Pair of golden dancers. $68.00

Mexico Sterling costumed dancers.
Silver, stone-accented maracas.
$135.00 (pair)

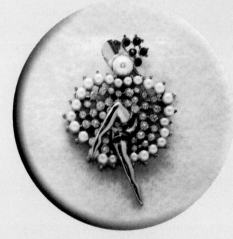

Kramer cancan dancer.
Has lavender rhinestones on her hat and garters.
Has pearl face, skirt is edged with pearls. $145.00

Alice Caviness, from Germany.
Sterling silver dancer, set with
marcasites. $98.00

Art Nouveau show girl.
Marcasite and sterling silver.
Onyx face, headpiece is a coiled snake.
$165.00

Sterling musician with lute.
Diamanté, green, and blue rhinestone
decoration. $134.00

Bob Mackie.
Mardi Gras dancer. $110.00

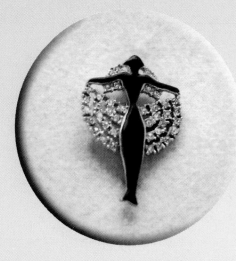

Art Nouveau dancer, enamel and pavé. $75.00

Male dancer awaits his partner. $30.00

Dancer in black enamel tutu. $32.00
Fan becomes part of the dance. $45.00

Dancer in blue enamel tutu lined with
rhinestones. $20.00
Floral skirt in pastel colors graces this
dancer. $25.00

Ballet skirt has blue rhinestones with
diamanté bodice. $35.00

Female dancer with rhinestone head
and bodice. $45.00
Male ballet dancer with pearl face. $55.00

Flamenco dancer.
Polka dot dress. $85.00

Square dance couple on a
scarf holder. $28.00

Entwined dancing couple. $68.00

Dancing ballet couple.
Faux-turquoise petal acccents. $85.00

Reja ballerina. $160.00
Tortolani ballerina. $85.00

Bali dancer on bed of pearls.
$68.00

Golden prima ballerina. $72.00

Costumed Dutch folk dancers.
Made from embroidery floss.
Comes with matching earrings. $65.00

Russian Cossack dancers.
Each figure is jointed in the middle.
$48.00 (pair)

Art Deco 1930s dancer. $84.00

Dominique "Ginger and Fred."
Made of flexible chain links with
preset rhinestones. $95.00

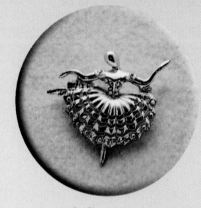

Swarovski crystal jewelry.
Annual edition, "Joy." $250.00

Jasper ballerina in dainty
diamanté costume. $35.00

Mardi Gras dancers, chatelaine.
$78.00

Spanish dancers, chatelaine. $65.00

Chinese dancers, chatelaine. $45.00

Bob Mackie vaudeville dancer.
$78.00

Hollywood Tahitian drummer.
$38.00

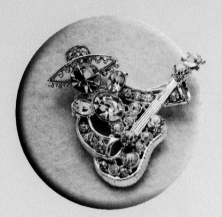

Napier troubadour.
Faceted, purple rhinestone guitar. $78.00
Jomaz jester.
Red enamel face. $175.00

Strolling troubadour in silver
and diamanté. $8.00

Nordic Sterling strolling musician with
vermeil face and accents. $135.00

Snake charmer.
Pearl and rhinestone accents. $32.00

Blue moonstone harem pants
bedeck this drummer. $32.00

PEOPLE FROM AROUND THE WORLD

Eisenberg Original king and queen
chatelaine fur clips. $965.00

Gene Verracchia mask.
Made by Gem Craft. $105.00

Creslu royal court lady from the
days of Camelot. $85.00

Garrison peasant lady. $58.00

Sterling silver king. $88.00

Knight of the court with
imitation-ivory face. $135.00

Sterling silver Spanish señorita wears her prized possessions: hair comb and fan. $85.00

Norma formal couple with red rhinestone faces, sterling. $165.00 (pair)

Green-eyed court jester. $38.00

Boucher native. Six emerald-cut glass stones in sombrero rim. $875.00

Marbel SC Aztec parure, marked "Mexico." Brooch, earrings, necklace, and ring. $175.00

Mexico Sterling boy and girl earrings. $65.00

Aztec tribal mask with turquoise
accents. $55.00

Mexican at siesta. $28.00
Arab with scales. $34.00

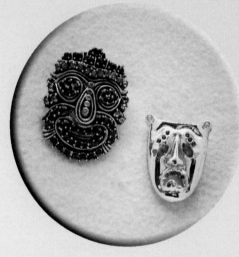

Aztec ritual mask done in rhinestones. $60.00
Theatrical tragic mask. $18.00

R.B.Z. sterling, made in Mexico.
Native girl with swaying skirt. $64.00

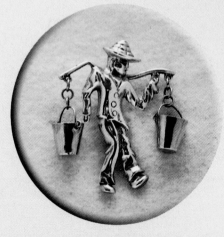

Taxco Sterling
Mexican water carrier. $88.00

Mexican peasant couple. $65.00

Egyptian figure, head is surrounded by four
Bakelite arrows. $58.00
Sterling vermeil girl in blue and white
pleated skirt. $45.00
Blackamoor in harem costume. $65.00

Joseff turbaned man in gold plating.
Drop earrings, finished in antique gold,
feature three heads. $400.00

Lisner Egyptian pharaoh
silverplated necklace. $76.00

Ciner blackamoor.
Rhinestone collar and hat. $125.00

Jeanne genie.
Pavé-studded turban. $49.00

Blackamoor chatelaine.
One brooch is full figure,
second has two faces. $105.00

33

Enamel warrior in yellow turban. $48.00
Curious Turk with blue crystal face. $68.00

Turbaned genie with red,
white, and blue accents. $38.00

1950s turbaned Turk. $58.00

Two turbaned genies with glass
"magic" crystals. $45.00 (each)

Rajah with faux ruby in turban. $82.00

Turbaned sheik. $64.00

Blackamoor earrings.
Pair on left has turban with long earrings.
$45.00 (pair)
Pair on right sports a crown. $35.00 (pair)

HAR trousered genie with glass ball. $275.00

Turbaned Turk brooch with earrings. $135.00

Reinad Far East royalty.
Ornate crown, bejeweled rhinestone
earrings and gown. $285.00

Tara Egyptian princess with
ornate head piece. $38.00

Louis Viale deposé fur clip, Paris,
woman in stylish dress. $195.00

Coro pieces.
Hand with polished fingernails, faux diamond
ring, and emerald bracelet. $275.00
Turbaned African. $45.00

Marvela Egyptian necklace.
Has two strands. $65.00

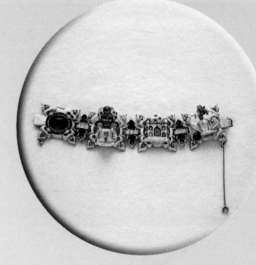

HAR figurals.
Harem eunuch carries crystal with a faux ruby. $340.00
Harem girl with fish-bearing crystal. $275.00
Soothsayer with magic ball. $156.00

HAR Taj Mahal bracelet. Charms include genie,
magic crystal, and Aladdin lamp. $1,150.00

HAR figurals.
Lariat necklace. $185.00
Brooch with matching earrings. $450.00 (set)

Trifari.
Collar of green, red, and blue glass stones.
Turban ends in a pavé trail. $195.00

HAR gentlemen.
Blackamoor has diamanté earrings. $260.00
Maharaja is decorated with seed pearls. $195.00

Hobé oriental woman. $300.00

Robert costumed man. $375.00
Monet oriental lady. $65.00

Asian girl bracelet with matching earrings.
$110.00 (set)
Male and female natives, in full headdress,
are double sided. $85.00

Napier smiling Chinaman necklace. $85.00
Monet fur clip monarch pin. $105.00
Napier smiling Chinaman head. $70.00

Marvella temple attendant. $78.00
Trifari fairy princess. $48.00

CoroCraft pieces.
Coolie carrying water. $305.00
Maiden wearing hat. $85.00

Weiss Chinaman brooch and earrings.
Coppertone with gold rhinestone accents. $165.00

ART Bali temple maiden. $50.00

ART Japanese, carrying lantern and
lovebirds. $48.00

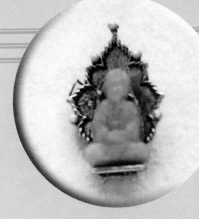

Ambassador Peking glass
Buddha. $58.00

Oleg Cassini oriental maiden. $98.00

The two faces of China in
this reverse carving of Con-
fucius and Mao. $48.00

Inca god in enamel costume. $78.00

Temple maiden. $82.00

Chinese coolie fur clip, sterling silver. $78.00

Cinnabar Buddha brooch. $105.00

Balinese temple attendant, faux ruby earring and emerald head piece. $88.00

Chinese Mandarin. $75.00

Buddha temple brooch with Peking glass. $58.00

Balinese goddess with green glass earrings. $80.00

Chinese ceremonial actor. $42.00

African maiden wearing
her wealth. $48.00

Bali mask, sterling silver. $78.00

Asian couple, plastic.
Woman with pearls and crown. $35.00
Coro man with crown. $28.00

Risa Japanese maiden
under cherry tree. $78.00

HAR pieces (clockwise from 12 o'clock).
Full figure, pot-metal brooch. $275.00
Parure containing: chain bracelet with
single charm (hanging from full figure brooch),
small brooch, larger brooch (bust only), and earrings. $1,400.00 (parure)
Bust brooch (in lighter color) and matching earrings. $525.00

Reinad oriental god medal. $185.00

Red plastic native ring. $24.00
Selini Indian maiden bracelet. $48.00

Hirsch Spanish señorita. $84.00

Italian policeman. $48.00

Mongolian tribesman, enamel. $80.00

Young Russian girl in ethnic costume. $68.00

Sterling silver Cossack. $55.00

Hattie Carneige head hunter. $285.00

Dawun Copper, made in South Africa.
Mother and babe. $75.00

Kirschenbaum tribal maiden. $80.00

African tribal women chatelaine. $48.00

African headsman, ivory. $95.00

Figurals

Hand-painted mask brooches.
$35.00 (each)

African mask earrings. $25.00

Young African tribesman. $54.00

African natives with Bakelite drums.
Medicine man.
Maiden with mirror.
Bongo player.
$85.00 (each)

African women portraits.
$40.00 (each)

African woman with
braided-rope hair. $32.00

Germany.
African native woman in tribal
headdress and earrings. $85.00

Selro Corp blackamoor parure.
Bracelet, lariat necklace, and earrings. $295.00

Selro Corp parure.
Necklace with three double-image
charms and two faux-ivory tusks and
matching earrings. $98.00 (set)

Selro Corp parure.
Ring with pink native-head stone. $48.00
Bracelet with pink native heads and faux-ivory
tusks, earrings match. $125.00 (set)

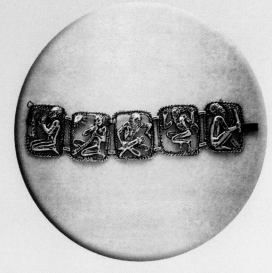

Seva, marked "Australia" and the word "Carroboree"
(which means wild native dance). Links portray
Aboriginal musicians and dancers. $105.00

Chanel profile pin.
Rhinestone top knot and
cheek, hat trimmed with
diamanté rhinestones. $650.00

45

Polcini court jester.
Gold-plated chatelaine,
pavé ruffle. $135.00

Chanel native in palm tree. $850.00

FANTASY AND LEGEND

Tortolani necklace.
St. George the dragon slayer.
$200.00

Eisenberg Original "Big Bad Wolf" in
grandma's clothing. $1,100.00
Hattie Carnegie old man of the sea riding
faux-jade fish. $210.00

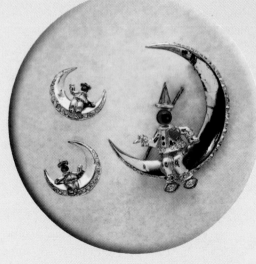

CoroCraft sterling.
Man on the moon with matching
earrings. $350.00

Korda Aladdin riding his
magic carpet. $74.00

Kirks Folly "Mad Hatter." $64.00

BSK.
Four o'clock scholar. $55.00
Fawn with lyre. $48.00

JJ Merlin and Excalibur. $78.00

Jack in the box necklace (lever on
side pops him up). $40.00

Gingerbread man necklace, enamel. $38.00

Jack and Jill fur clips. $95.00 (pair)

1930s Jack and Jill fetching a pail
of water, enamel. $140.00

Retread tire man. $48.00

Jack and Jill water carriers. $95.00

"William Tell." $64.00

"Mr. Magoo," enamel. $78.00
School girl with a pearl face. $65.00

"Hopalong Cassidy" brooches.
"Hoppy" mounted on horse at Bar XX Ranch. $85.00
Break-away gun reveals HC's name inside. $68.00

Peking glass Buddha. $58.00
Vale Stevens zodiac crab. $48.00

Joseff sun god.
Diamanté rhinestones
dangle behind the open slots of his
eyes. Matching earrings not shown. $325.00

Joseff necklace has six antique gold chains
with slide that features a young maiden
wearing a grape garland. $800.00

Tortolani Taurus key chain. $35.00

Tortolani pieces.
Water maiden's stones are cabochons. $105.00
Aquarius is silverplated. $78.00

Tortolani zodiac grand parure has bracelet, necklace,
small brooch, and earrings. $1,400.00

Coro Bacchus mask.
Black enamel with diamanté trim. $695.00

Diana Love (by Trifari) necklace.
Black head of Zeuss, with faux-jade drop,
on four-strand, golden chain. $285.00

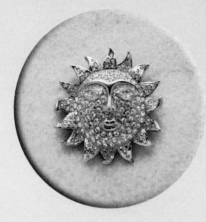

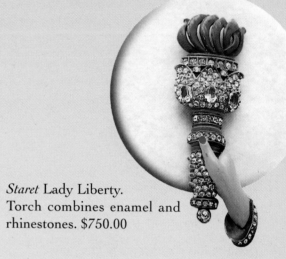

Staret Lady Liberty.
Torch combines enamel and
rhinestones. $750.00

Carol Lee sun god. $68.00

Boucher jester fur clip.
Pull the chain and his legs and arms move!
$5,000.00

Sterling by Cini Gemini brooch.
$80.00

Tortolani pieces.
Water-maiden necklace. $85.00
Silverplated mermaid. $90.00
Pendant mermaid has a ribbed chain
tail that is flexible. $98.00

Tortolani pixies.
Enamel pixie rides the pearly crescent
moon. $175.00.
Silverplated pixie has delicate wings. $150.00

Ledo "Wednesday's Child" bracelet,
marked, "1958." $65.00

Coro September birthstone bracelet. $65.00
HAR English bobby, white enamel, blue hat. $90.00

Korda wizard from Baghdad.
$58.00

Edgar Berebi ruffle-collared Pucchini
sits on crescent moon. $78.00

Korda wizard from India.
$78.00

51

ART snowman with golden
top hat and scarf. $38.00

Kirks Folly snowman. $92.00

Bauer snowman with black
rhinestone accents. $125.00

Ceramic pixie girl and boy,
hand painted. $45.00

Scarecrow man. $42.00

Accessocraft wizard. $54.00

Jointed robot has emerald-cut
pink belly stone. $46.00

Neptune with his trident. $18.00

Google-eyed pineapple people.
$30.00 (pair)

Cupid with upswept hair, brooch
and matching earrings. $86.00

Kirks Folly fairy castle. $68.00

Oleg Cassini mermaid. $85.00

Jolle fairy dancer with flower hat
and skirt. $55.00

Fairy dance of the flowers.
Brooch and earrings. $85.00

King of hearts. $48.00

Heart headdress on
pot-bellied native. $28.00

Opera singer (perhaps Faust?).
Full stage make up, plastic. $52.00

Weiss political pins.
Democratic donkey.
Republican elephant.
$150.00 (pair)

Kenneth Jay Lane Santa Claus
holiday pin from the Franklin Mint. $145.00

ART Santa with a
bag of gifts, enamel. $42.00

Fabric Santa Claus. $28.00

Gerry laughing Santa. $28.00

Dominique Santa Claus.
Beard is pre-set, link chain,
rhinestones. $85.00

Kramer Santa.
Frosted white and red
with pavé face. $125.00

Hollycraft elongated Santa pin.
Faux-emerald belt buckle,
pearl-trimmed costume. $85.00

Weiss identical Santas.
Red and white enamel. $65.00
Gold plated. $80.00

Joseff cuff bracelet and necklace. Embellished with charming cupids, amethyst rhinestones, and pearls. $975.00

Boucher leprechaun carrying a pearl. $95.00
Boucher angel holding garland. $85.00
Joseff cupid necklace with red and green glass beads and tear-drop pearls. $450.00

Tortolani cherub with curly hair. $78.00
Eisenberg Ice snowman with shovel. $65.00
Tortolani scarecrow with pavé accents. $65.00

Hattie Carnegie Cupid readies his bow. $225.00
Hattie Carnegie little girl peeks over the fence. $175.00
Joseff angel riding the crescent moon. $375.00

Jomaz Peking glass Buddha. $135.00
Florenza Cupid has a gift-wrapped heart. $90.00

Tortolani "Voice of Conscience."
Perch one on each shoulder to display
your angelic or devilish mood. $225.00

ART praying angel. $38.00

Kirks Folly romantic angel. $62.00

Kirks Folly lucky-penny angel.
$68.00

Sterling by Lang flying angel. $75.00

Kirks Folly celestial angel oversees
the moon and stars. $74.00

Kirks Folly neck-
lace. Angel's rise
from the ocean. $58.00

57

Celeste angel brooch. $18.00

Kirks Folly caroling angels. $68.00

AJC angel with watering can. $38.00

Artifacts (by JJ) swinging angel. $34.00

Yarn angel. $18.00

Kirks Folly lyre-playing angel. $48.00

Red enamel devil with
forked tail. $45.00

Red devil. $34.00
Gold devil. $18.00

Spain hand-painted devil.
Red devil has long tail, pitchfork,
and pearl head. $55.00

Ultra defiant devil.
This sitting satan appears to be
sticking out his tongue! $22.00

Coro charm bracelet.
Each Biblical character depicts a different
commandment (ten in all). $85.00

Buddha necklace with coral beads. $45.00

Animals

BARNYARD

Proud cock of the walk. $84.00

Blue-belly rabbit with trembling carrot. $78.00
Celluloid rabbit with flowers. $48.00
Blue rooster with rhinestone accents. $65.00

Alvaire pride of the barn yard
in full plumage. $68.00

Hobé bird pins.
Silver owl with gold-plated eyes. $45.00
Mexican chicken with green rhinestone
eye. $62.00

Hobé silver donkey. $50.00
Boucher gold-tone rabbit. $98.00

KJL faux-pearl-bellied pig. $90.00
Napier rooster. $48.00

Coro Sterling rooster. $165.00

R. Mandell lamb.
Wool is made of small gold rings
anchored to body and head. $105.00

Warner chick. $78.00

Pauline Rader gold-plated rooster.
Orange, marbled, pear-shaped, stone
belly. Full tail feathers. $115.00

Ciner donkey proudly packs his
load of rhinestones. $64.00

Jeanne crowing roosters.
Enamel rooster has red rhinestone comb. $65.00.
Gold-tone rooster has a musical tail! $74.00

Cyna donkey's large green ears allow him
to hear all the stable gossip. $54.00

Jeanne gold-plated Arkansas
razorback boar. $38.00

Juliana 1950s articulated donkey.
$110.00

Capri blue rooster,
japanned finish. $54.00

Denmark enameled rooster. $55.00

Giovanni gold-plated rooster. $48.00

Oleg Cassini barnyard fowl
has faux-turquoise belly.
$90.00

This little *BSK* chick wears his rhinestone, Sunday best. $34.00

JJ cow didn't jump
over the moon! $34.00

Silverplated charging bull with
rhinestone accents. $24.00

Gold-plated donkey is sitting
down on the job. $38.00

Donkey watch brooch. $47.00

Colorful rhinestone bunny head. $35.00

This bunny has found a large blue egg. $48.00

Peter Cottontail (pearl), gold plated. $22.00

Green and amethyst rhinestones
create this bunny's body. $75.00

White enameled snow bunny
tries out skis. $40.00

Little plastic lamb has red heart
and pearl tail. $38.00

Lucite enamel cow still has charm
after fifty years. $185.00

Baseball bunny. $28.00

Juliana running rabbit. $145.00

ART blue enamel mule shows his
best profile. $28.00

Sterling silver bunny with lucite
jelly belly. $105.00

Trifari animals.
1990s jelly-belly rooster. $145.00
Rabbit. $35.00

Mimi di N golden pig belt buckle,
1973. $65.00

Tortolani pieces.
Toothy rabbit. $38.00
Ski bunny with pearl tail. $45.00

Hobé lamb has chain top knot. $150.00
Mazer pearl-eyed rabbit. $80.00

Original by Robert enamel roosters in white
and green. $90.00 (each)
Mylu rabbit with rhinestone-studded
bowtie. $60.00

DOGS

Jomaz darling pup has red glass nose. $95.00
Monet bowing poodle is ready to play. $48.00
Jomaz precious pooch has pavé mustache. $80.00

Trifari poodle with pavé body and
head. $35.00
HAR enamel basset hounds in red
berets. $40.00 (each)

Marvella poodle coiffed in pink
enamel flowers. $78.00

R. Mandel Yorkie has chain hair. $88.00
Panneta dancing poodle has poseable head.
$125.00

Pauline Rader poodle.
Seed-pearl top knot, green
rhinestone eyes. $78.00

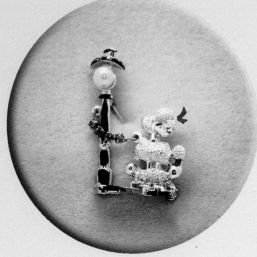

"Fifi" waits at the pearl lamp light. $29.00

JJ poodle has gold-tone body and
textured hair. $40.00

Disney Dalmatian. $65.00

Dogs with personalities.
Danson gold-plated pup with
rhinestone eyes. $46.00
LG bloodhound prepared to run away.
$46.00

Germany poodle charm bracelet. $55.00

Capri poodles.
Black rhinestones. $60.00
Red rhinestones. $65.00

BSK dog pin.
Gold-plated overlay sits on large,
red glass stone. $48.00

BSK rhinestone poodle. $38.00

Artifacts (by JJ) Dachshund on original, dated card. $38.00

Esteé Lauder 1992 Scottie. Opens to reveal solid perfume. $95.00

Plastic enamel dog proudly boasts "New York 1939." $80.00

Embarrassed Scottie in blue enamel bow. $70.00

"Where's the fire?" Plastic, 1930s. $68.00

Resin beagle with amethyst glass mouth. $12.00

Rattail chains create the
illusion of hair. $475.00
Chain used to form hair on articulated dog
necklace. $45.00

Pair of classy poodles.
Silverplated. $15.00
Red rhinestone prancer. $28.00

Dolled up for the evening
in real mink. $19.00

Pooch in pink enamel cap
and bow. $25.00
Gold-tone dog in diamanté
collar. $28.00

Silver overlay transforms two
purple stones into a dog. $38.00

Silverplated dog,
rhinestone ears. $19.00

Poodle has rhinestone ears
and top knot. $18.00

Articulated, gold-plated
poodle necklace. $65.00

Gold-plated poodle with blue tail. $24.00
Silverplated poodle with ridges. $18.00

Bright red plastic terrier with
moveable head, 1940s. $54.00

Stylish poodle with rhinestone
accents. $65.00

Florenza blue pin-cushion,
rhinestone poodle. $75.00

Rattail chain Pekingese. $45.00

Copper-tone dog. $22.00

Dalmatian hand-carved agate
necklace. $55.00

Long-legged rhinestone poodle. $85.00

Enamel poodle with
diamanté collar. $48.00

Silver-tone pup with blue
teardrop ear. $28.00

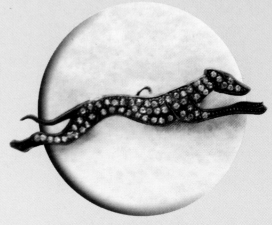

Sleek Greyhound, 1930s. $58.00

Panneta gold-tone bloodhound. $55.00
Trifari gold-tone and green enamel hound. $38.00
Trifari faux turquoise and blue navette accents. $68.00

Enamel boxer. $22.00

Schreiner of NY poodle, brown
rhinestone. $125.00

Holiday Poodles.
Mylu gold-plated pup wears a bright
Santa hat. $45.00
Original by Robert gray pooch sports
a red cap and collar. $78.00

Joseff poodle brooch. $285.00
Hattie Carnegie dog. $110.00

KJL Scottie. $85.00
Boucher poodle. $80.00

CATS

Diamanté kitty plays with pearl ball.
$75.00
Green-eyed cat with diamanté
collar. $68.00

Coro pewter cat. $175.00
Napier silver cat. $25.00

Joseph Warner gold-tone kitty with soft
blue rhinestone accents. $38.00

Hollycraft cat, pastel
cabochons. $80.00

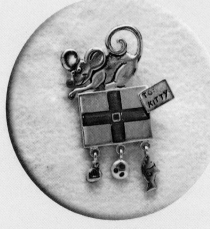

Tara mouse on giftbox. $38.00

Dodds dark green cat with pink collar and ears.
Earrings repeat the pattern. $60.00

Lea Stein Paris.
Red cat with ball. $275.00

Sterling silver cat with large
blue glass stone. $95.00

JJ gives their cat brooches personality.
Big-eyed scholar. $28.00
Playful kitty. $25.00

Burmese mesh cat with tiger-eye
stones. $105.00

Frosted pink enamel kitty. $14.00
Black flow epoxy cat. $25.00

Uptown golden cat. $25.00
Lavender faux-marble cat. $18.00

Gold-plated kitten with large eyes. $35.00
Winking cat has milkstone body. $24.00

Twin kittens in different colors.
$95.00 (each)

Blue rhinestone cat with
black whiskers. $38.00
Felix the cat. $78.00

Purple cat. $20.00
Pair of peridot cats. $45.00

Danecraft black cat has his own
Halloween lantern. $48.00

Spring-mounted tail on this cat
trembles. $48.00
Red rhinestone collar accents this
diamanté cat. $28.00

Jeanne cat dangles his mouse catch
on a silver chain. $38.00

LJM, blue stone chips fill in the belly
of this cat. $38.00

Ciner kitty has ball of
diamanté yarn. $56.00

AJC kitten checks out his reflection. $23.00

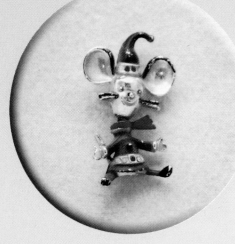

BJ Christmas mouse in
full elfin attire. $22.00

Ciner winking kitty. $38.00

JJ version of Halloween cat
and pumpkin. $48.00

JJ cat and dog shown in
traditional pose. $25.00

AJC kitty caught in automatic
washer. $28.00

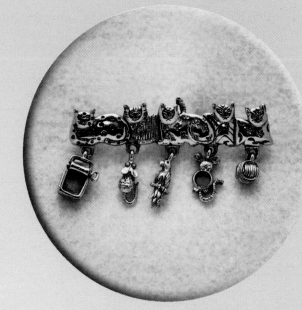

AJC kittens with their
special toys. $32.00

JJ cats check out the fish bowl.
Silver. $30.00
Gold. $27.00

Florenza black cat with diamanté collar
featuring "13" in red rhinestone. $90.00

Diamanté cat
with red rhinestone
collar. $30.00

Winking cat, articulated
filigree necklace. $35.00

JJ version of hobo mouse.
$38.00

LG enamel hobo.
$35.00

Schreiner of NY mouse is small,
but has lots of rhinestones. $45.00

Golden mouse has a flexible tail. $12.00
Rhinestone green and pink mouse. $28.00

Avon mouse has adjustable
glasses. $24.00

11 W. 30th St. satin-finish cat with rhinestone
eyes, nose, and ears. $8.00
Trifari white enamel cat with matching
earrings. $125.00
Coro gold-plated cat. $34.00

HAR friends.
Pink-eared mouse has pink bow
on tail. $75.00
Pink-eared cat is playing with blue ball
of yarn. $60.00

Tortolani cats.
Scared cat. $95.00
Meow for your dinner. $68.00

Mylu mouse with Christmas tree. $38.00
Castlecliff mouse with green belly stone. $50.00
Alice Caviness blue-bellied cat with green eyes. $82.00
Alice Caviness cat with dark red rhinestones. $95.00

Cat and mouse pair,
gold-plated with flexible tails. $12.00 (each)
Cheerful mouse with pink enamel body. $18.00

KJL diamanté mouse with faux-pearl
nose. $78.00
Lisner, cat with green enamel. $38.00

Hobé golden kitty with large brown belly
stone, 1969. $75.00
Hattie Carneige dancing cats. $195.00

Joseff green-eyed cat parure.
Brooch, necklace, and earrings. $950.00

HORSES

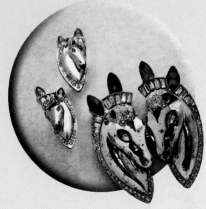

Coro sterling horse duette with
matching earrings. $425.00

Ciner bright red equine with gold
rhinestone trim. $65.00
Napier stallion with rhinestone-
studded mane. $45.00
Panetta gold-tone prancer. $98.00

Trifari horses.
Satin-finish profile with emerald-green eye. $95.00
White enamel with gold accents. $140.00

Trifari jelly-belly with English saddle. $450.00

Kramer satin-finish filly with chain tail. $95.00

Prancing horses chatelaine. $68.00

Elizabeth Taylor for Avon, 1980s.
Pearl and pavé accents. $145.00

Gene Verrecchia.
Limited edition, 2000. $65.00

Axcess horse and rider.
Made in Great Britian, pewter. $95.00

Esteé Lauder rocking horse.
Contains solid perfume, 1998. $95.00

Silverplated, saddled,
rhinestone horse. $38.00

Lucite-based horse head,
studded with rhinestones. $78.00

Little racer with rhinestone accents
and sapphire eye. $45.00

Horse head with red rhinestone eye and
antique gold-plated finish. $75.00

Scatter pins of the 1940s.
Pair of young foals. $25.00

Made in England Sterling silver
race horse with jockey. $145.00
Gerry silverplated reindeer with
green holly bow. $28.00

Trifari pavé horse with blue
baguette saddle. $48.00
Pavé horse and rider enjoy
English fox hunt. $135.00

Sterling silver jockey riding gold
vermeil horse. $225.00

CoroCraft sterling donkey has vermeil finish,
diamanté and red baguette mane,
and red navette ears. $150.00

Hattie Carnegie donkey with load of pink and
blue beads. $175.00
KJL long-eared donkey with pavé mane and
emerald-green eyes. $74.00

IN THE FOREST

Panagopoulos Dina leaf cuff. $265.00

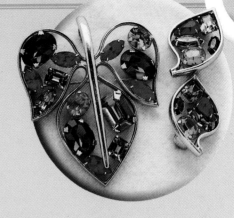

Napier fall foliage brooch and
earrings. $145.00

Judy Lee silver brooch and earrings
with gold accents. $65.00

Satin-finish leaf. $48.00
Alice Caviness marcasite-accent foliage,
made in Germany. $65.00
Original by Robert yellow acorn with
green cap. $48.00
Original by Robert black-capped
mushroom. $55.00

Weiss fall foliage.
Green enamel leaves with matching earrings. $95.00
Brown enamel leaves. Matching earrings,
same design as green, not shown. $60.00

Castlecliff pieces.
Enamel quail. $65.00
Porcupine with quills. $50.00

H. Pomerantz of NY leaf,
aurora borealis. $38.00

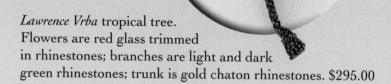

Lawrence Vrba tropical tree.
Flowers are red glass trimmed
in rhinestones; branches are light and dark
green rhinestones; trunk is gold chaton rhinestones. $295.00

Natasha sterling vermeil
rabbit chatelaine. $145.00

Nettie Rosenstein tree branch fur clip. $170.00
McClelland Barclay golden leaf covered by
pavé top leaf. $285.00

Silver oak leaves and acorns. $98.00
Mexico Sterling hollow-heart
earrings. $45.00

UR Creations oak-leaf pin and earrings
with acorns and pavé accents. $85.00

Monet ram's-head ring. $28.00

Danecraft bunny gardener in pink pinafore and hat. Note a bird bath and sprinkling can as props. $78.00

Ernest Steiner Original acorn-eating squirrel has diamanté tail. $105.00

Little brother pavé bear. $54.00
Big brother has matching gold bow and gold-plated nose, hand, and foot pads. $85.00

Flexible, poseable, pavé buddies.
Gold-tone bunny has jointed arms and legs. $85.00
Large teddy also has a moveable head. $90.00

Lea Stein (Paris) pearlized fox. $150.00

Capri mushroom with blue and
purple rhinestone cap and
enamel stem. $48.00

ART gold-plated squirrel
heads for his winter storage
with rhinestone acorn. $38.00

Edgar Berebi "Teddy Bearebi."
Limited edition pin with magnetic
tummy and three costumes. $110.00

Edgar Berebi "Beatrice."
Limited edition, jointed pin.
Also comes with three costumes. $110.00

Sarah Ann Coventry winking bunny.
Note design technique on his ears.
$28.00

Sarah Ann Coventry brooch and earrings.
Beautiful deer-in-forest scene.
Silver plated. $65.00

Danecraft honey bear. $38.00

Stanley Hagler forest tree
in full bloom. $85.00

Karu 5th Ave. rhinestone rabbit.
$58.00

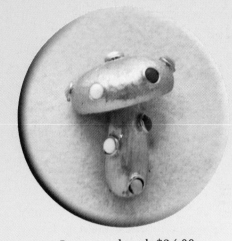

Jeanne toadstool. $24.00

Gerry forest denizens.
Brown enamel squirrel. $18.00
Brown enamel bear cub. $18.00

Esteé Lauder snail opens to sachet
perfume. $25.00

Barclay squirrel with pink
opaline stomach. $28.00

Matching silver-tone deer heads.
$12.00 (each)

Avon teddy bear sachet
necklace. $34.00

Bellini ferret with dark red
rhinestone "stripes." $38.00

Catskill Game Park Inc., Catskill, New
York. Fall woodsy scene with running
stag. $80.00

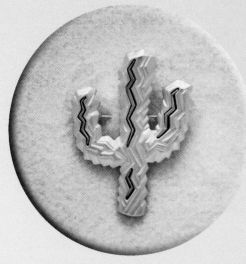

JJ cactus in gold and silver tones. $24.00

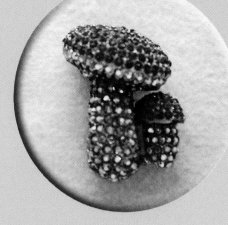

Rhinestone mushroom fur clip. $45.00

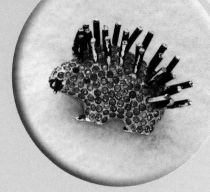

Porcupine has red rhinestone eye
and prickly quills. $82.00

Two acorn-bearing squirrels.
Tiny, gold squirrel has pavé
accents. $18.00
Larger, silver-tone squirrel has pink
rhinestone body $60.00

Raccoon bandit with multifaceted
"amethyst" belly stone. $58.00

"Flower. "
From Walt Disney's *Bambi*. $65.00

"Foxy-loxy" black enamel fox
with rhinestone accents. $75.00

Pair of chipmunks
preparing for winter. $45.00

Toadstool has a
diamanté cap. $24.00

Gold-plated squirrel admires the choice
acorn. $18.00
Adorable chipmunk gives a toothy
smile. $38.00

Tortolani wind-swept tree. $195.00
Howard Pierce deer. $180.00

ART leaf pin with insect. $48.00

Boucher bear has Peking glass body and pavé
accents. $95.00
Boucher squirrel has a turquoise tummy
and accents. $105.00
Hobé fox has turquoise eyes. $35.00

BIRDS OF FLIGHT AND FANTASY

Wooden-bead necklace forms
home for two yellow brids.
Matching earrings not shown. $30.00

Boucher love birds hover over pavé nest
filled with eggs (pearls). $1,500.00

Boucher diamanté stork. $900.00

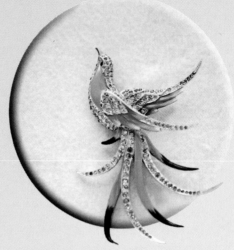

Boucher bird flaunts blue enamel
and pavé feathers. $410.00

Boucher birds.
Roadrunner. $55.00
Toucan. $85.00

Boucher birds.
Blue-capped bird with dark blue
rhinestones and pavé accents. $340.00
Gold-winged bird with dark red
rhinestone breast. $125.00

Boucher duckling with trembler head. $78.00
Hattie Carnegie gooney bird, plastic. $110.00

Boucher pavé birds. $1,300.00 (pair)

Vendome birds.
Enamel toucan. $110.00
Pastel-colored tropical bird. $88.00

Jomaz birds.
Pavé chicadee on branch. $78.00
Resplendent peacock in full array. $200.00

Reja peacock with orange crackle-look stone. $175.00
ART songbird in bright enamel. $24.00
ART parrot with large yellow cabochon. $55.00
ART parrot in bright enamel. $48.00

Coro hummingbird has trembling wings. $150.00
Napier chick has white enamel belly. $48.00
Original by Robert cardinal in beautiful red enamel. $65.00

Chanel turkey. $325.00

Eisenberg gold-plated eagle with explosions of rhinestone stars in the background and pearl in his claws. Earrings are stars and pearls. $875.00

Trifari gold bird with diamanté baguettes. $350.00
CoroCraft sterling and enamel pheasant. $295.00

Coro birds.
Georgeous lovebirds with diamanté trim. $425.00
Royal peacock with aurora borealis stones. $48.00

Weiss peacock brooch and earrings in red, blue, and amethyst diamanté. $185.00

95

Siver-tone eagle with sparkling
pavé and baguettes. $38.00

Trifari barn swallows.
Light blue moonstone body repeats in
matching earrings. $100.00
White faux pearl and red cabochon. $70.00
Dark blue stone on larger bird. $85.00

Kramer opaline songbird earrings. $48.00
Panetta pavé roadrunner. $84.00
Panetta songbird. $64.00

11 W. 30th St. jeweled birds.
Pink stones outline wings and cape, green
stones adorn tail feathers, eye, and beaks.
Design is repeated in red and blue.
$48.00 (each)

Parrot scatter pins, sterling silver. $135.00

Kramer birds.
Enamel-winged bird with black onyx head
guards her nest of pearl eggs. $180.00
Gold-tone bird with pearl body rests on a
branch. $58.00

Pell bird with long rhinestone-studded tail
feathers. $74.00
Puccini peacock with sapphire cabochons.
$98.00

Marvella dove with olive branch. $68.00
Mitchel Maer opaline hummingbird. $55.00

Judy Lee silver bird.
Edge of large wing, branch, and tail
feathers have rhinestones. $35.00

Kramer of NY exotic, diamanté bird
with sweeping wings. $160.00

Sterling pheasant with green enamel
wings. $68.00

Swarvoski chickadee, pavé. $68.00

Warner golden-beaked bird. $56.00
Vogue JLRY red-breasted bird. $45.00

Marcasite peacock with blue, green,
and red rhinestone accents. $95.00

Rafelian enamel blue bird. $58.00

Scitarelli feathered friend.
Blue cabochon belly has overlay of gold
on wing. Tail feathers are custom-made
rhinestones. $74.00

Rafelian enamel eagle. $85.00

Red, white, and blue eagle in full flight. $88.00

Seagull ring. $25.00

Bejeweled peacock. $38.00

Rhinestone turkey. $16.00

Sterling silver peacock with green-glass feather accents. $63.00

Royal peacock, 1930s.
Perch is pink/blue baguettes. $95.00

Multicolored rhinestone peacock
with a Siamese flair. $85.00

Tourmaline body is the focal point
of this peacock. $48.00

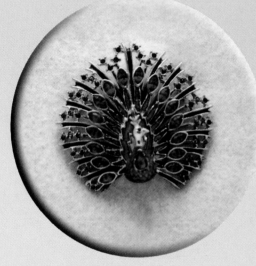

R. J. Graziano peacock.
Green enamel body, red and green
rhinestone feathers. $55.00

Puccini peacock.
Pavé feathers and sapphire
blue accents. $65.00

Trifari jelly-belly bird.
Reintroduced in 1990s. $70.00

Jeanne gold-plated brooch.
Nest houses pearl eggs.
Comes with matching earrings. $85.00

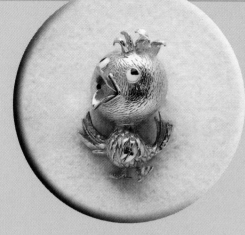

Ciner chirping chick. $60.00

Florenza flip-top bird.
Opens to reveal small bowl for saccharine tablets.
Comes with tiny tongs. $78.00

Swallow brooch and matching earrings,
sterling silver. $75.00

Spotted, enamel owl. $53.00

Proud eagle has red, white, and
blue rhinestones. $63.00

Two friends share a branch. $32.00
Large-beaked, silver pelican with pink
and green rhinestones. $38.00

Two birds cooing on perch. $28.00
Small bluebird guards her nest of
pearl eggs. $30.00

Yellow-bellied bird with pearl eye. $30.00
Inquisitive bird with two large amethysts. $75.00

Bluebird hovers over pearl egg
on tree branch. $38.00

Pink-bellied lovebirds. $35.00
Trio of birds. $38.00

Green bird has three glass stones. $32.00
Crowing rooster has round, yellow belly. $18.00

Turquoise-bellied, gold-plated bird. $65.00

Ready for a night on the town,
with top hat and cane. $62.00

Lovebirds on heart silhouette,
1930s. $35.00

Silver rooster. $10.00
Bird in flight. $18.00

Newly-hatched chick
with pearl egg. $34.00

Two versions of popular humming birds.
Gold plated with rhinestone eye. $38.00
Silverplated with pink belly. $25.00

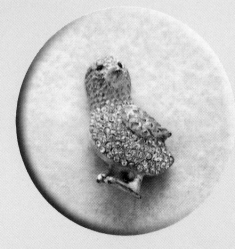

Gold-plated rhinestone chick. $38.00

Cadora partridge in a pear tree.
This company didn't usually
use enamel. $185.00

Cadora doves (9) form a
golden tree. $225.00

Silken bluebirds painted
on metal back. $95.00

Eagle necklace.
Note large faux topaz in center. $44.00

Have you ever seen
a fuchsia swallow? $86.00

The color of your dress will become the wing
and tail color of this golden bird. $38.00

France heart brooch.
Two loving parents feed their hatchling.
Marked, "Made in France." $265.00

Southwestern version of the Phoenix.
Faux turquoise and coral accents. $48.00

Black and white enamel swallow.
Wings are spring-set tremblers. $68.00

1930s bird fur clips perch on the
shoulders. $200.00 (pair)

Eagle brooch with full spread wings.
Comes with matching earrings. $48.00

Two rhinestone chicadees share
red rhinestone cherries. $74.00

Topaz bird has pearl feet. $32.00

Ready to take flight. $42.00

MJM stork has a surprise. . .

"Look, I am a lapel watch!" $68.00

Faux-turquoise hummingbird. $38.00

Navette glass stones are used
to create this bird. $55.00

Original Dejay parrot.
Made of yellow enamel, 1940s $130.00

Beckman.
Color has gone to the head
of this sterling bird with red and blue
cabochons. $48.00

Plastic parrot
has matching earrings. $80.00

Colorful enamel bird with bright
blue rhinestone eye. $40.00

Flow enamel gives an
almost cloisonne appearance
to this tropical bird. $48.00

Bird perches on a goblet. Sterling with
lavender, vermeil feathers. $48.00

Sterling bird with lavender,
vermeil feathers. $34.00

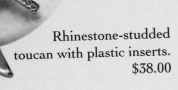

Rhinestone-studded
toucan with plastic inserts.
$38.00

1930s enamel Art Nouveau bird
with flowing feathers. $68.00

Coro lyre bird with enamel accents.
$995.00

Coro colorful lovebirds brooch with
matching earrings. $95.00

Burmese bird of mesh,
enamel feathers. $98.00

Rhinestone-studded bird on perch. $48.00

Mitchel Maer hummingbird with rhinestones
and opaline cabochons. $78.00

Plume of diamanté feathers
is a sight to behold! $65.00

Bob Mackie uses his
eye for color with feathers
of fuchsia rhinestone and green
enamel. $105.00

Diamanté royal bird cage with faux pearl
and golden bird. $48.00

This bird of diamanté and
enamel has her own house. $68.00

Two birdbath pins with rhinestone
accents. $55.00 (each)

Darling birdbath and birdhouse
pins with pink enamel decorations.
$65.00 (each)

Coro enamel peacock
fur clip. $95.00

Trifari birds.
Exotic, gold bird with flowing tail feathers. $180.00
Exquisite silver bird with pavé accents. $155.00

CoroCraft brooch.
Square-cut topaz glass belly, pavé
body, and enamel beak and tail
feathers. $395.00

CoroCraft sterling stork, head trembles. $395.00
Coro enamel pelican, aurora borealis eyes
and pavé trim on wings. $145.00

HAR chirping bird, red enamel with
faux-pearl belly. $63.00
HAR congenial crow, black and yellow enamel
with white "halo." $54.00
Christian Dior ('67 Germany) Colorful bird with
fuschia cabochons and enamel. $200.00

CoroCraft pieces.
Soft green enamel ostrich, sterling. $195.00
Sterling stork. $145.00

Bird necklace has two
birds in nest, five (on charms)
below nest, and one dangling. $32.00
Coro enamel-winged swallow has faceted belly stone. $25.00
Coro gold-plated swallow has red rhinestone eye. $55.00

Silson enamel bird brooch,
made in Canada. $140.00

CoroCraft gold-plated beauty with diamanté
accents and ruby baguettes. $175.00
Coro duette lovebirds. $225.00

Trifari bird of paradise,
reintroduced in 1990. $125.00
Weiss enamel toucan. $75.00

Coro birds.
Diving swallow has green-glass belly and enamel
accents. Comes with matching earrings. $65.00
Sterling lovebirds pin has lovely leaf details. $125.00

CoroCraft sterling birdbath $225.00
Coro turquoise blue peacock. $48.00

Castlecliff enamel pheasant. $68.00
Eisenberg Original emerald green
glass dove. $350.00

Tortolani pieces.
Fledgling has seed-pearl body with pavé tail. $80.00
Sand seagulls in black and green. $110.00
Road runner. $90.00

Red-bead necklace with enamel parrots.
Comes with matching earrings $78.00

KJL pieces.
Turquoise-breasted bird has
enamel feathers and pavé cape. $80.00
Larger bird has pavé head and back, and
enamel breast. $135.00

Wooden-disc necklace with yellow parrots
and matching earrings (not shown). $55.00

Inlaid parrot necklace with
pearlized beads, pearls, carnelian,
and black beads. $175.00

Parrot close up.

Reja stork.
Polished gold
and pavé stripes. $295.00

Boucher Phoenix.
This exquisite pavé bird has gorgeous
red and green enamel feathers.
Serious "bling!" $2,700.00

Boucher birds.
Pavé and pearls in a striking array. $475.00
Turquoise-breasted bird. $260.00

Coro white enamel bird duet. $38.00

Hobé chick is breaking out
of his shell. $155.00

Boucher birds.
Phoenix is splendidly accented in pavé and
rhinestone. $375.00
Eagle has lucite jelly belly and green
rhinestone eye. $45.00

Italy necklace.
Hand-blown, glass doves with holly
leaves and berries.
Matching earrings not shown. $145.00

Eisenberg diamanté eagle has miniature eagle earrings. $850.00

Black flamingo with palm trees. $150.00
Silver stork with pavé tail feathers. $68.00

Charel pheasant in flight. $65.00

WATERFOWL

Tortolani swans.
Smaller bird has glass stone and
diamanté accents. $75.00
Larger bird has faux-jade belly and
"fluffed" wings. $125.00

KJL penguin with top hat and cane. $85.00
Pennino stork with top hat and cane. $225.00

Trifari white enamel duck with green rhinestone eyes
and gold accents. $145.00
Mazer pin-tail duck with enamel and
rhinestone feathers. $225.00

Coro birds.
Enamel flamingo. $295.00
Sterling jelly-belly swan. $350.00

Small enamel penguin. $18.00

Three penguin tie tacs, with ice blue
rhinestone bodies. $18.00 (trio)

Sterling swan with cabochon
body and wings. $68.00

Swan has her signet trio on her chatelaine. $75.00

Male and female penguin fur clips. $95.00

Penguin in black tuxedo has faux-pearl belly. $65.00
Penguin in white tuxedo has glass topaz belly. $68.00

Cini pelican.
Tag reads, "Contra Brand."
$128.00

Flamingo, pink rhinestone body with
lavender enamel wings. $68.00

Topaz-colored penguin has gold wings and pavé vest. $52.00
Diamanté penguin has dark rhinestone accents. $38.00
Umbrella-carrying penguin has smooth moonstone belly. $48.00

Penguin brooches.
Mom carefully watches her brood.
Fledglings answer her call. $75.00 (set)

Sterling silver duck with
rhinestone collar. $85.00

Long-legged stork with pavé wings. $55.00

Enameled duck has his
umbrella handy. $43.00

Pelican dangles his fish catch. $325.00

Swarovski swan. $58.00

Aurora borealis stork. $48.00

Sterling silver large-beaked bird,
green glass stone. $58.00

Swan with lime green body
and silver wings. $28.00

Green glass duck duo brooch. $68.00

Small pavé chick. $38.00
Sterling silver duck has rhinestone
baguette wing. $65.00

Silver swans. $35.00 (pair)

Top hat duck. $85.00

Pavé stork with multicolored feathers. $48.00

Sterling silver duck has blue faceted-glass body. $75.00

Swan lake beauty with tiara. $78.00

Oleg Cassini pelican guards three pearl eggs. $64.00

Red plastic flamingo. $75.00

Pavé swan features square-cut
rhinestone body. $68.00

Large diamanté swan with touches of black
enamel on feet, beak, and eye. $84.00

Pavé flamingo. $74.00

Trio of golden ducks. $20.00
Two-ducks brooch. $65.00

Contemporary swan in modern
rhinestone settings. $28.00

Ducks-in-flight chatelaine. $80.00

Pair of ducks. $54.00

Pre-set, link-chain rhinestone swan. $68.00

Trifari blue-bellied duck. $68.00
Coro blue-bellied swan. $95.00
HAR enamel penguin. $95.00

CoroCraft pieces.
Seahorse duet with green rhinestones. $325.00
Penguin has topaz glass belly. $395.00

Eisenberg Ice swan with blue rhinestones. $75.00
Monet gold-plated duckling. $45.00

Coro pieces.
Gray swan. $145.00
Aurora borealis duck. $38.00

Trifari birds.
White enamel signet swan. $165.00
Golden duckling. $60.00

TORTOISES AND TURTLES

Tortolani, Crislu turtle necklace. Head
hooks onto shell. $150.00

KJL turtles.
Sea turtle with enamel pink and lavender shell. $110.00
Turtle with large, blue cabochon body. $95.00

Napier gold-plated turtle. $28.00
Razza articulated turtle necklace. $78.00
ART yellow and orange enamel turtle. $42.00

HAR pieces.
Red glass-bellied turtle. $35.00
Enamel turtle with pink bow. $44.00
Turtle with faux-turquoise, pearls, and rhinestone. $65.00

Original by Robert turtles.
Enamel land turtle. $76.00
Green enamel sea turtle. $80.00

Warner turtle with two purple stones. $55.00

Kramer turtle with blue faceted-glass belly. $80.00
Hollycraft turtle with colorful pastel cabochons. $85.00

Whiting & Davis turtle necklace, silver plated with large domed cabochon. $65.00

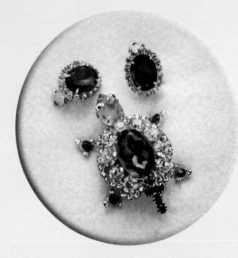

Juliana brooch and earrings.
Large, multifaceted glass stones dominate this set. $225.00

123

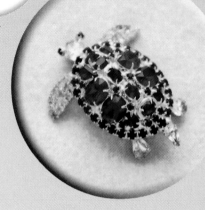

Ciner white-shell tortoise. $58.00

Bauer turtle studded with red rhinestones. $68.00

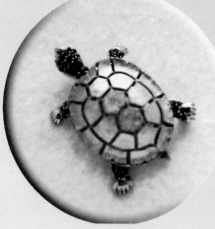

Ciner tortoise with rhinestone accents. $54.00

Alan turtle necklace. $45.00

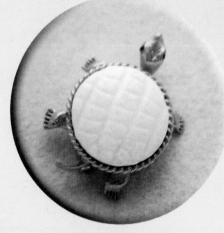

Polly Bergen hard shell.
A limited quantity of these turtles were available for a short period of time. $95.00

Jeanne turtle shell has metal work imitating the real thing. $45.00

Jeanne turtle leaving home with
his hobo sack. $45.00

Jeanne green cabochon turtle. $54.00

Jan tortise, coral beads stream
across the shell. $65.00

Erwin Pearl turtle has a traveling
black-ribbed shell. $60.00

Lanvin Paris turtle with brown enamel shell
and green cabochons. $58.00

De Nicola turtle in green enamel
floral costume. $78.00

LG raised-enamel turtle. $38.00
Emmons turtle with square-cut center
and ring of pearls. $25.00

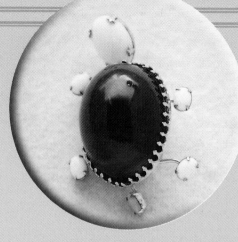

Schreiner of NY turtle travels with white
feet and head and a cabochon shell.
$125.00

Green faux-malachite shell and
green chatons. $52.00

Diamanté head, legs, and tail frame
large, faceted-glass stone. $110.00

Interlaced green and rust
cabochons form shell. $40.00

1930s sterling silver vermeil serves as frame
for emerald green glass stone. $60.00

Shell highly decorated with diamanté and green and blue chatons. $45.00

Silverplated turtle. $30.00

Lavender navette glass encircled with lavender chatons and square-cut amethyst. $75.00

Gold-plated turtle with red and pink rhinestone. $18.00

Tourmaline cabochon shell. $28.00

Enamel shell resembles a hat. $28.00

Pink charms all that see her. $32.00

Light and dark green shell. $48.00

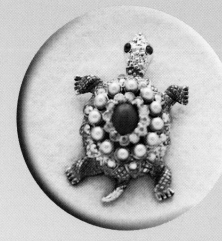

Pearly shell with green cabochon center. $24.00

Topaz rhinestone shell. $38.00

Schreiner of NY turtle in lavender and purple. $135.00

Topaz cabochon with golden knobs. $49.00

Coro sea turtle with dark red
rhinestone-trimmed shell. $195.00

Pell turtle has one band of diamanté
across top of shell. $75.00
Coro jelly-belly turtle fur clips. $425.00

Mimi di N brown enamel turtle with faux-turquoise
shell and pearl clusters. $145.00
HAR gold-tone turtle with large "crackle"
cabochon shell and tiny turquoise accents. $65.00

KJL faux-coral turtle with
redstone shell. $65.00

HAR turtles.
Enamel turtle has faux-coral shell under gold bars. $70.00
Faux-turquoise cabochon and small beads. $55.00

FROGS

Original by Robert enamel frog and lily pad. $95.00
Tortolani green-bellied bull frog. $125.00
Monet silver frog with green eyes. $45.00

KJL parure.
Seven-frog bracelet, clip earrings on card,
and a brooch with watch that can be seen
when back is lifted. $475.00

Weiss frog with large,
faux-amber stone. $140.00

Mimi di N link necklace is golden jumper
with Peking glass eyes. $350.00

Weiss toad with green warts. $85.00
Mazer frog with blue-glass body. $98.00

Made in Mexico shoulder sitter has lavender
and amethyst rhinestones. $95.00

Swarovski faceted emerald green
glass belly. $74.00

ART enamel frog.
"Are you smiling?" $52.00

ART frog.
Ready to croak. $48.00

SAC pavé frog with green
cabochon eyes. $38.00

Jeanne pair of jumpers. $45.00 (each)

Swarovski black frog with
golden flowers. $80.00

131

LG enamel green hobo. $32.00

Faceted red-glass stone. $35.00

Bauer green leaper. $82.00

Butler & Wilson English frog prince. $89.00

Jeanne frog with egg-shaped body. $30.00

Pavé trio.
Little one. $48.00
Big brothers. $95.00 (each)

Pavé frog with green leg stripes and eyes. $28.00

Small turquoise frog on lily pad. $58.00

Plastic frog with rhinestone accents
on arms and legs. $48.00

Free-form frog done in various
shades of blue and red. $16.00

Same frog in light green. $18.00

Gold frog with green rhinestones. $18.00

Pavé golden frog with emerald green eyes. $35.00

Gold frog with pink and gray enamel bands. $42.00

Golden frog has large, green stone in his brooch. $18.00

Bright green fiddler. $10.00

Unusual, copper-tone frog. $55.00

Gold frog with bright red hands and feet and lucite belly stone. $42.00

Two-tone green jumper with
pavé hands and feet. $45.00

Jointed frog in silver and green. $16.00
Enamel tree frog in green and gold. $28.00

Trifari frogs.
Small frog has blue glass body with green
glass and diamanté legs. $75.00
Large frog has green and gold enamel body
and red rhinestone eyes. $98.00

Eisenberg blue enamel frog is actually a pendant. $125.00
Renard vermeil frog has topaz belly stone. $195.00

Joseff bronze frog on green
lily pad. $225.00

OWLS

CoroCraft sterling triple-owl fur clip. $480.00
Coro fur clip owl duo. $195.00

ART green bellied owl has topaz eyes and
pavé top knot and feet. $45.00
Reja sterling owl has pear-shaped, faceted-
glass body. $145.00
ART owl is orange and yellow enamel. $42.00

E (Eisenberg) enamel owl necklace. $125.00

Joseff silver pewter-finish owl necklace. $295.00

Razza sleepy owl necklace. $85.00

Tortolani silver owls.
Startled bird. $45.00
Traditional pose. $38.00

Nettie Rosenstein owl necklace has
a large creamy belly. $295.00

Trifari owls.
Small, gold owl has
red rhinestone eyes. $68.00
White enamel owl has yellow and
clear rhinestone accents. $130.00

Weiss owls.
Enamel owl is brightly colored
in yellow and red. $55.00
Rhinestone owl comes with matching
earrings. $135.00

Hollycraft owl with orange
rhinestone belly. $76.00

Link chain, orange chaton owl has large,
faceted-stone belly. $95.00

Tailored owl, matte gold finish. $30.00
Green navette owl has aurora borealis
outlines. $58.00

Gold, twisted-rope cage
becomes owl's belly. $35.00

Owl pendant has large, round belly. $30.00
Gold owl has beautiful blue eyes. $18.00
Scholarly owl has large green belly. $30.00

Owl necklace with frosted green navette body. $44.00
Silver owl has pearl eyes and pavé hood. $32.00

Gold-plate owl has large carnelian
tummy. $22.00
Pygmy owl has green faceted-stone
tummy. $58.00
Large owl has three large, clear
navettes. $65.00

Pearl-bellied owl has enlarged eyes. $18.00
Antique gold owl perched on branch. $45.00
Golden owl. $35.00

Owl necklace has overlapping layers of metal feathers. Comes with matching earrings. $65.00.

Small, silverplated owl has brilliant red stone and diamanté accents. $18.00
Large-eyed owl has pearl and aurora borealis breast. $28.00
Sterling silver owl has beautiful peridot eyes. $62.00

Enamel duet, twin scatter pins. $40.00 (pair)

SAC owl with pearl egg and accents. $18.00
De Nicola winking owl with one red eye. $48.00
De Nicola gold-plated owl with turquoise breast. $54.00

Owl-head necklace opens to reveal solid perfume. $38.00

Owl brooch has pearl eyes and rhinestone accents. $34.00

Silver, hinged owl necklace. $48.00

Milkglass navette owl pendant. $48.00

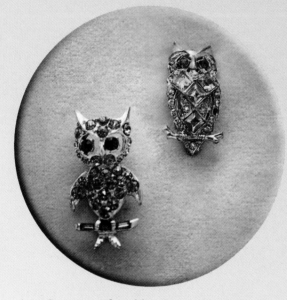

Green-eyed owl has lovely lavender
rhinestones. $65.00
Pink-eyed owl has diamond-shaped
diamanté. $28.00

Small owl necklace has red
rhinestone body. $38.00
Silverplated owl has red "crackle-
stone" body and eyes. $28.00

Gold-plated owl with emerald eyes. $24.00

Owl necklace. Rows of golden loops create
three layers of feathers. $45.00

JJ owl has personality! $30.00

Beau Sterling owl with large faceted-stone eyes and white enamel. $95.00

Avon owl holds solid perfume. $24.00

Silver silhouette necklace. $35.00

Goldette necklace features alternating layers of silver and gold. $39.00

Swarovski pavé owl is gold plated. $64.00

141

Glass stone picks up colors of green
and blue enamel. $48.00

White enamel owl. $22.00

This owl has bold enamel stripes
on his head. $22.00

Green and blue enamel compliment
this green-eyed bird. $34.00

Sarah Ann Coventry red-eyed golden owl.
Eye glasses are adjustable. $28.00

Jeanne sleepy owl sports large,
faceted faux-topaz tummy. $35.00

Wise old owl in spectacles. $22.00
Owl head is loaded with pavé stones. $18.00
Red and black rhinestones adorn this bright-
eyed fellow. $35.00

Silverplated necklace.
Small owl dangles from chain. $38.00

Coro owls.
Two-owl brooch comes with teal
blue earrings. $350.00
Topaz-eyed owl has pavé accents. $70.00

Original by Robert owl has enamel head and wings
and small green and blue cabochons. $110.00
Alice Caviness necklace in shades of brown. $80.00

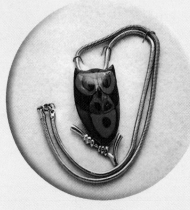

Original by Robert bright enamel owl. $75.00
Monet blue-eyed, silver owl. $52.00

Eisenberg enamel Picaso. $185.00

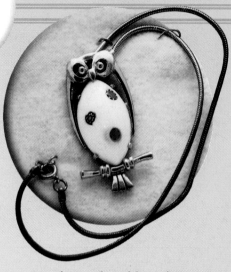

Eisenberg owl necklace. $78.00

Florenza owl, head bends backward to reveal a cigarette lighter. $85.00

SNAKES, LIZARDS, AND SPIDERS

CoroCraft Sterling enamel lizard carries pearl egg. Diamanté top ridge. $995.00

Trifari critters.
Green chameleon. $54.00
Satin and polished gold-plate snail. $90.00

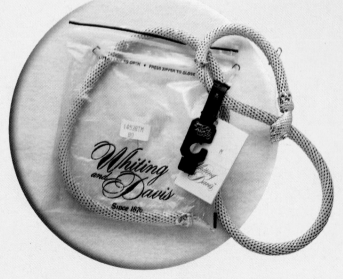

Whiting and Davis metal snake belt. $68.00

Katherine K by Norma Jean.
Coiled snake. $45.00

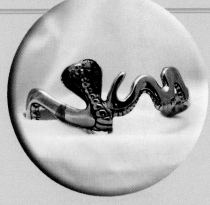

Cos sterling cobra bangle. $92.00

Whiting and Davis coiled mesh snake bracelet started a fashion fad. $65.00

Rhinestone spider crawls on faux black rock when pearl chain is pulled. $185.00

Czechoslovakia multicolored cabochon stones. $48.00

Black widow spider. $35.00
Silver spider with blue stripes. $18.00

Czechoslovakia spiders.
Silver spider with rhinestone accents. $35.00
Cabochon-stone spider. $32.00

Snail sports large red cabochon back. $28.00

Nicky Butler sidewinder. $80.00

Spider chatelaine. $65.00

Spider and web chatelaine. $40.00

Trifari coiled cobra brooch. $80.00

ART cobra bracelet. $55.00

Emmons lizard. $35.00

Sterling silver lizard
with vermeil. $65.00

Red, white, and
blue snake. $38.00

Small golden lizard. $25.00

Rhinestone lizard with
chain garland, 1940s. $65.00

Red rhinestone
lizard. $45.00

147

Three diamanté rows run the
length of this lizard. $50.00

Red-eyed snake coils around light
green cabochon. $18.00

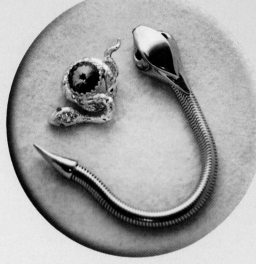

Navettes of various colors
adorn this lizard's back. $35.00

Small snake coils around green
watermelon stone. $24.00
Gold-plated cobra has red rhinestone eyes
and snake-chain body. Tail has sharp hook
to fasten into clothing. $45.00

Leaping lizard. $65.00

Butler and Wilson
shoulder-sitting spider. $225.00

ART snake with turquoise beads. $48.00

Trifari pieces.
Sterling jelly-belly spider. $575.00
Lavender glass-bodied fly. $450.00

HAR cobra parure.
Necklace, cuff, bracelet,
and earrings. $1,950.00

Pearl caterpillar. $28.00
HAR rhinestone lizard. $75.00

Tortolani designs.
Seahorse pendant
with jointed chain body. $95.00.
Gold-plated dragon necklace. $140.00

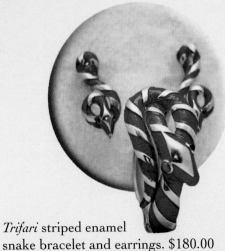

Trifari striped enamel
snake bracelet and earrings. $180.00

Original by Robert
snake belt, mesh. $135.00

KJL faux-coral spider. $98.00
Kenneth Lane rhinestone spider. $75.00

Trifari sterling pavé lizard
with six black beads. $105.00
KJL enamel lizard with pavé head.
Marked, "China." $65.00

ART snake trio and earrings. All have
red, forked tongues. $110.00

Snake bracelet with
sapphire eyes. $34.00

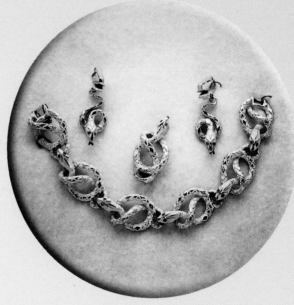

ART snake parure.
White enamel bracelet, brooch, and earrings.
All have red, forked tongues. $145.00

KJL two-headed snake bracelet. $80.00

Eisenberg Ice spider $350.00

INSECTS

R. Mandel bug with glass
cabochon. $105.00

Hattie Carneige bee has trembling wings. $85.00
Hattie Carneige, trembling wings flutter over the
body. $95.00
Austria faux-turquoise bug with matching
earrings. $78.00

Hobé insects.
Opaline flyer. $75.00
Delicate bee. $64.00

Napier ladybug with
pearlized body. $60.00

151

Kenneth Lane blue turquoise dragon fly. $125.00
KJL gold bug. $65.00

Beetle has topaz and green glass body. $75.00
Enamel flower wings overlay this bug's orange body. $48.00
ART winged grasshopper with opaline cabochon. $65.00

Kenneth Lane beetle, three shades of green
rhinestones on wings and neck. Blue baguettes
on head and body. $98.00

Hobé faux-coral dragonfly. $68.00
KJL for Avon enamel-winged dragonfly
with rhinestone body. $85.00

Joseff beehive.
Assortment of brooches and matching earrings. $475.00

Coro enamel bee has trembling wings. $78.00
HAR caterpillar rests on yellow enamel leaf. $75.00
Sandor enamel daisy has tiny butterfly. $84.00

Original by Robert white enamel flower
with ladybug. $98.00
Lily pad provides a place for
two ladybugs. $68.00
Monet leaf with insect. $78.00

Vendome enamel dragonfly.
$110.00

Alice Caviness, pink enamel wings over
a pink stone. $65.00
Regency, japanned-finish aurora
borealis stones. $75.00
Eisenberg, topaz belly with gold wings
and head. $55.00

Trifari pieces.
White enamel bee with blue wings. $48.00
Sterling vermeil fly with pavé wings. $160.00

HAR pieces.
Large fly with
wings of both polished
and satin-finished gold. $55.00
Ladybug has lovely pavé center and raised, gold dots. $55.00
Art Deco bug is brightly colored in orange and yellow. $48.00

Trifari designs.
Sweater guard (with chain) has
matching earrings. $68.00
Gold-plated brooch. $78.00
Enamel brooch. $180.00

Trifari white enamel bee with gold
wings and beads. $52.00
Weiss enamel beetle with peridot
rhinestones. $65.00

Trifari insects.
Blue-eyed fly with faux-
pearl body and pavé head. $55.00
Faux-turquoise winged dragonfly. $42.00
White enamel beetle with turquoise beads. $48.00

Weiss bug pins.
Large fly, green enamel
wings overlay green emerald-cut glass. $70.00
Fat fly has peridot rhinestones and glass stone accents. $85.00
Blue bug has japanned, iridescent glass body and head. $50.00
Beetle has pink enamel with green peridot rhinestones. $68.00

Trifari jelly-belly fly with
earrings, sterling. $750.00

Monty Don fly has flat back, royal blue
wings, red head, and rhinestone tail. $68.00
Weiss fly is yellow and green enamel. $75.00

Trifari enamel scarab necklace. $85.00

Warner turquoise bug, chained
to clip-on leaf. $65.00

TJ fly has trembler spring wings
and bright glass body. $58.00

Swarovski foil glass, stone-
bellied bee. $75.00

Zental enamel bee. $48.00

Warner aurora borealis bug. $48.00

Made in Mexico shoulder-sitting grasshopper with diamanté stones. $74.00

Kramer flyers.
Enamel bee. $95.00
Enamel firefly. $80.00

Warner imitation-scarab body with enamel leaves. $38.00

Polcini three-layer beetle necklace has a swiveling head. $75.00

Joan Rivers pavé bee scatter pins have matching bee earrings. $89.00

Reinað diamanté insect, banded with blue rhinestones, 1930s. $160.00

Gorgeous bee has sterling wings and body with pear-shaped, faceted amethyst glass stone. $95.00

Sterling enamel insect. $78.00

Pair of snails hang from double chains in this chatelaine. $68.00

Tatiana Faberge firefly. $55.00

R. J. Graziano firefly. $58.00

Jeanne red-stone bee. $28.00
Gerry silver and black bee. $18.00

Sadie Green blue-stone bug. $68.00
Reja Sterling bee with amethyst stone. $195.00
Cini small silver-winged insect. $72.00

De Nicola bee. $74.00

Swarovski honey bee. $68.00

Joan Rivers bee brooch with
matching earrings. $58.00

Bavarian Art Glass blue lady bug.
Made in Canada. $38.00

Jeanne hobo caterpillar with knapsack.
How fast do you think he will go? $54.00

Sterling by Cini bee hive
comes complete with bee. $98.00

Jeanne turquoise, ruby, and aurora
borealis rhinestone bug. $54.00

Rena Lange black bat. $26.00

Beau Jewels gold-plated trim on
enamel leaf on which a tiny
rhinestone-eyed bug perches. $44.00

Bonetto diamanté bee will always be on time.
A novel lapel watch. $48.00

Ledo blue faux-turquoise beads form body
of bug sitting on veined leaf. $85.00

Capri red enamel lady bug. $42.00

B. *Blumenthal & Co. Inc.* beetle with
opaline wings. $98.00

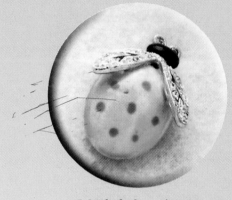

BSK lady bug. $48.00

Ciner eye-catching, pearl-
wearing insect. $54.00

Ciner white enamel bee. $85.00

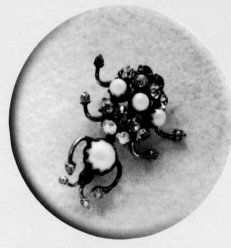

Avon firefly with four-strand pearl tail. $22.00

Schreiner of NY bug with faux pearls
and smoky rhinestones. $80.00

Flocked, striped bee with cobweb wings. $22.00
Pavé-striped bee with pink navette wings. $19.00

Trembler wings with blue navette rhinestones
and small pink chatons. $65.00

Beehive key ring. $16.00

Enamel snail. $28.00
Gold-plated caterpillar. $22.00

Bee scatter pins, emerald body and
golden wings. $45.00 (pair)

Faux-pearl dragonfly with rhinestone wings. $22.00
Spider scarf pin. $15.00
Rhinestone dragonfly with red navette wings. $68.00

Insect with matching earrings.
Green glass body, gold stone wings. $58.00

Gold-plated beetle with rhinestone body,
comes with matching earrings. $35.00

Faux-pearl fly with pavé head and wings. $38.00
Large pavé fly. $22.00

Gold-tone fly has blue enamel wings. $25.00
Silver-tone fly has blue teardrop body and
light blue navette wings. $22.00

Gold-plated bug with topaz glass tummy
and cool blue eyes. $28.00
Dark-winged fly has amber, pear-shaped
body. $19.00

Sterling silver insect with
amethyst glass body. $85.00

162

Two enamel beetles. $24.00 (each)

1930s brown enamel beetle. $78.00

White enamel wings. $38.00

Soft green and blue navettes. $32.00

1930s speciality two-tone glass body has
silver overlay wings. $85.00

Green cabochon-winged bug. $22.00
Enamel firefly. $16.00

Enamel firefly. $48.00

Blue scatter pins. $28.00 (pair)

Metal-winged insect. $32.00
Geometric insect. $38.00

Gold bug has pavé stomach and smoky
topaz wings. $20.00
Green cabochon bug has dainty,
teardrop wings. $18.00
Gorgeous amethyst bug has a pearl
head. $18.00

Two scatter pins have open wings,
matching earrings. $48.00

Cabochon scatter pins with
matching earrings. $55.00 (set)

Scatter pins have cabochon body and
navette wings. $30.00 (pair)

White metal butterfly has wings that tremble. $95.00
Rhinestone fly has sterling silver wings. $38.00

Baguettes, navettes, and chatons in pink
and purple bee. $175.00

Silver spiders with brilliant teardrop bellies. $28.00 (pair)

Multicolored, tiered cabochons give
this fly an appealing look. $45.00

Pink trembler, double-deck pink wings. $55.00

This opaline bug is accented with
aurora borealis stones. $45.00

Golden firefly is fastened to material by pinching wings. Comes with matching earrings. $65.00

Fiddling grasshopper with rhinestone violin. $110.00

Pot-metal enamel, 1930s grasshopper. $138.00

Multicolored rhinestone, 1930s. $95.00

Rhinestone grasshopper in beautiful shades of blue and green. $48.00

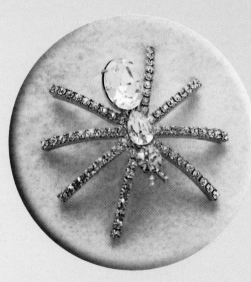

Shoulder-sitting diamanté spider. $55.00

Faceted rhinestone forms the unusually large body of this fly. $65.00

Trio of diamanté bees on rhinestone chain necklace. $78.00

Schreiner of NY snail. $95.00

Praying mantis, 1930s, white metal enamel. $135.00

Magnifying glass necklace with enamel bee guardian. $45.00

Topaz-winged fly has pearl accents. $48.00
Turquoise-winged fly has faux-pearl tummy. $34.00

Weiss bugs.
Gold rhinestone tie tac. $28.00
Gold-tone bug with black stone belly. $85.00
Blue rhinestone bug with tremble wings. $85.00

Coro pieces.
Red-eyed, enamel bee fur clips. $95.00
Gold-tone enamel bee duette. $350.00
Large fly with faceted green glass body. $395.00

Original by Robert black and white enamel fly. $58.00
Monet fly crawling on leaf. $78.00
Monet silver fly. $55.00

Coro black enamel bee. $45.00
CoroCraft sterling fly with
rhinestone wings. $85.00

Original by Robert
dragonfly in yellow
and black. $78.00
Monet bee. $38.00
Original by Robert green
enamel grasshopper. $64.00

BUTTERFLIES

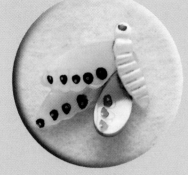

Celluloid butterfly. $45.00

Hobé ceramic butterfly necklace. $150.00

Austria butterfly with green and
blue rhinestone. $65.00
Hattie Carnegie butterfly with faux-
turquoise stones. $98.00

Boucher butterflies.
Two butterflies form this unique brooch.
One in silver hovers on trembler spring
over black butterfly. $280.00
Multicolored rhinestones and faux-turquoise
accents adorn this dainty butterfly. $125.00

La Roca brooch and earring sets.
White enamel outline is filled with
aurora borealis and red rhinestones. $95.00
Gold outline is filled with rhinestones in shades of blue. $155.00

11 W. 30th St. gold-plated butterfly. Turquoise-studded wings are accented with scalloped, pavé row. $65.00

La Roca butterfly with orange, citrine, diamanté, and green rhinestones. Earrings to match. $130.00

Vendome japanned, dark green pin comes with earrings. $150.00

ART butterfly with pearl, turquoise, and gold beads. $95.00
Vendome butterfly with bright enamel colors. $80.00

La Roca rhinestone butterfly sets. Orange and brown. $150.00 Shades of green. $135.00

Inlaid butterfly, black bead necklace.
Matching earrings not shown. $225.00

Closeup shows detailing.

Miriam Haskell plumed butterfly. $125.00

Monet wire butterfly with pearl
accents. $38.00
Napier white enamel butterfly. $65.00
Napier rhinestone butterfly in shades
of blue. $75.00

Napier silver butterfly with filigree
body and detailed wings. $295.00

Hattie Carnegie necklace, lavender
cabochons, red body. $750.00

Regency pieces.
Champagne/gold and burgundy/red.
$85.00 (each)
Shades of green and shades of blue. $105.00

More *Regency* pieces.
Smaller pins in pink, red, and blue/green. $85.00
Large blue pin. $105.00

Regency trio.
Shades of blue with pearl accents. $74.00
Japanned finish, comes with matching
earrings. $180.00
Shades of orange. $85.00

Alice Caviness quartet.
Pretty in pink. $135.00
Brilliant in blue. $80.00
Fashionable in fall colors. $95.00
Fabulous in fucshia. $95.00

Valfran Brody-Baiardi.
Sterling butterfly with amethyst body stone.
Matching earrings have lavender rhinestones. $175.00

Weiss butterflies.
Pastel, has earrings (not shown). $225.00
Pink enamel and rhinestones, with
earrings. $145.00

Sterling from Norway butterfly,
blue satin cloisonne. $120.00
Butterfly with blue, black, and white enamel. $68.00

Weiss butterfly in two shades of
pink with earrings. $225.00
Kramer butterfly in shades of brown,
with earrings. $185.00

Weiss duo.
Gold and red. $150.00
Red rhinestones set in japanned finish,
with earrings. $195.00

Weiss butterflies.
Blue, green, and red rhinestones. $95.00
Two red and pink japanned. $110.00 (pair)
Multicolored rhinestones. $155.00

Trifari set.
Satin finish, gold-plated set, with two brooches and matching earrings, features smokey rhinestone accents. $250.00

Trifari "flutter-bys."
Gold butterfly with satin and polished finishes. $58.00
White enamel butterfly with faux turquoise. $130.00
Same butterfly with faux coral. $130.00

Kramer stylized butterfly with diamanté navette body. $78.00

Trifari trio.
Amethyst rhinestones add a rich look to this lovely pin. $188.00
Polished-gold outline shows off diamanté rhinestones. $90.00
Peking glass stones are supported on green enamel wings. $165.00

Kramer sculptured, silver butterfly.
Tiny flowers have sapphire blue centers. $90.00

Yul Berynes 1986 unique pin. Small black butterfly rests on silver one's wing. $48.00

Ring with golden glass scarab. $25.00

Necklace and drop earrings with pink butterflies and flowers. $75.00

Matisse pin and earrings, copper overlay on enamel . $85.00

Esteé Lauder, filled with solid perfume (White Linen). $115.00

Link chain, pre-set rhinestones give this pin a fluid motion. Comes with earrings. $95.00

Ocean Treasures brooch and earrings. Sterling frame and shell flower petals. Even the butterfly wings are shell. $185.00

Kramer blue and green fur clip. $155.00

Thai scalloped butterfly in marcasite and onyx . $95.00

Hollycraft multicolored jewel. Decorated with pearls, rhinestones, and two gold-flecked glass stones. $125.00

Sterling silver set with marcasites. Colored rhinestones accent tips of wings. $170.00

Mabe, sterling silver with enamel accents, made in Germany. $95.00

Dominique nine-inch butterfly with purple cabochons, link chain, and pre-set rhinestone wings. $225.00

D'Orland, made in Canada. Pavé wings, red accents. $68.00

Juliana butterflies.
Orange and white. $65.00 (each)
Purple, pink, and green. $74.00

Juliana trio.
Green and blue glass navette. $85.00
Five colors. $64.00
Green, orange, and brown. $95.00

Austria beauty.
Sky blue glass stones in antique gold. $38.00

Trifari contemporary necklace and earrings. $85.00

ART butterfly.
Flowers can be found in
the upper wings. $62.00

ART highly decorated butterfly. $60.00

Juliana butterflies.
Small, shades of green. $94.00
Large, dark green stones. $165.00

Juliana "flutter-bys."
Light blue. $85.00
Dark blue. $135.00

Juliana duo.
Small butterfly. $85.00
Large butterfly. $140.00

Juliana, gold and green. $285.00

Juliana, shades of fuchsia and blue. $285.00

Juliana in the pink.
Earrings are exact copies
of upper wings. $395.00

Juliana butterflies.
Small, dark red. $95.00
Large, multicolored. $155.00

Juliana assortment.
Note the distinctive treatment
of the antennas. $90.00

Juliana butterfly brooch.
Body is a lemon-colored, square,
faceted-glass stone. $185.00

179

Cloisonne pendant on chain. $60.00

Golden butterfly necklace with blue beads
and green teardrop rhinestones. $65.00

Silver necklace with blue rhinestones. $30.00

Hand-painted brooches
with matching earrings. $68.00

JJ, enamel wings with pearl and
rhinestone accents. $35.00

Suzanne Bjøntegard,
"Made in England." $110.00

Butler & Wilson, made in England. Japanned finish enhances blue and fuchsia rhinestones. $145.00

Dominique pair in silver and gold. Diamanté and black rhinestones form wings. $48.00
Red rhinestones accent eyes and wing. $40.00

Butler & Wilson, English production. Scalloped glass fans. $195.00

Avon silverplated butterfly. $33.00

Navette pins.
Black and white. $68.00
White (milk) and clear. $65.00

John Hardy lapel clip, sterling silver wreath with butterfly. $85.00

The colors of fall give this butterfly
a natural appeal. $68.00

Diamanté body with faceted, foiled-stone
wings. Unique style, 1930s. $95.00

Japanned finish with accents in fall tones.
Comes with matching earrings. $65.00

Yellow, orange, and amber
rhinestone butterfly. Comes with
matching earrings. $70.00

Coral beads and orange wings contrast
beautifully on brushed gold. $38.00

Red butterfly duet chatelaine. $45.00

CoroCraft, vermeil wash over sterling silver contrasts nicely with green rhinestone navettes. $110.00
Nettie Rosenstein, sterling with Peking glass cabochons and diamanté accents. $140.00

Trifari, red rhinestones and pavé. $150.00
Weiss, blue rhinestones in gold wire. $110.00

Alice Cavniness, sterling, made in Germany. $98.00
Castlecliff trembler with cocoon. $125.00

Regency rhinestone butterflies.
Shades of green. $105.00
Topaz and orange. $125.00
Champagne and aurora borealis. $155.00

Judy Lee, pastel. $58.00
Shades of blue and green. $75.00

Monet, gold. $38.00
Original by Robert, yellow. $54.00
Original by Robert, pink. $65.00

UNDER THE SEA

Joseff seascape with coral gold fish. $285.00
Hattie Carnegie blue and coral plastic fish. $130.00
Kenneth Lane sea shell. $78.00

Green shrimp. $22.00
Capri starfish. $35.00
Godfrey Houston ceramic lobster. $24.00
Maine plastic lobster. $38.00

Reja enamel fish has pearl bubble. $295.00
ART enamel fish has lovely blossoms. $55.00

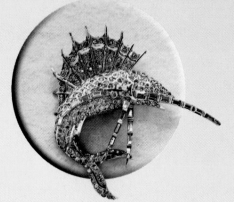

Boucher swordfish. $1250.00

Pillbox treasure-chest charm bracelet. $58.00
Boucher blue and green enamel starfish. $53.00
Boucher enamel angel fish. $68.00

CoroCraft sterling and enamel swordfish. $395.00
CoroCraft enamel coral reef. $75.00
Coro starfish. $28.00

Jeanne enamel sea horse. $95.00
KJL kissing fish. $65.00
KJL enamel fish. $95.00
Kenneth Lane octopus. $195.00

Vendome gold-plated sea horse with diamanté mane. $95.00
Monet white enamel, gold-ribbed fish. $48.00
Regency starfish with blue rhinestones. $80.00
Napier amethyst fish with gold ribs. $38.00

Monet silver fish blows rhinestone bubbles. $38.00
Coro fur clip clam shell. $30.00
Lisner gold fish. $28.00

Les Bernard
enamel octopus has won a gold star. $65.00
Alice Caviness pirate's treasure chest. $48.00

Alice Caviness fish.
Red-eyed gold fish and green-eyed version
both have "burr" scales and pearl dangles. $55.00 (each)
Small, enamel fish has marcasite trim. $78.00

Tortolani coral-reef brooch and
earrings, enamel. $45.00

Trifari, back to the sea.
Oyster shell has blue enamel branches
and pearl accents. $145.00
Seahorse is seated on pavé branch with
pearl accents. $195.00

Coro faux-pearl seahorse. $45.00
CoroCraft sterling silver, jelly-belly, enamel fish.
$395.00

Weiss pieces.
Enamel marlin has black spots and
red rhinestone eye. $55.00
Pink and red rhinestone starfish is
still on original card. $80.00

Trifari lobsters.
Gold plated. $90.00
Red enamel. $150.00

Trifari fish.
White enamel dolphin. $55.00
Sterling fish with cabochon belly. $125.00

Trifari fish.
Gold fish has a fancy tail. $110.00
Jelly-belly marlin was reintroduced
in 1986. $125.00

Lawrence Vrba pearl shell and coral
brooch. $300.00

Hollycraft fish with special pastel glass cabochons.
Fins and tail have golden bead outline. $80.00

P.I.M. pavé-accented lobster
holds a mabe pearl. $48.00
Artistically rendered gold fish. $35.00

187

Hollycraft red and clear rhinestone fish.
Gold burrs create the outlines. $178.00

Jan Michaels, San Francisco.
Charm bracelet has an assortment
of sea creatures. $145.00

Swarovski pavé octopus with gold outline
and blue cabochon eyes. $145.00

Vargas sterling vermeil swordfish. $84.00

Sterling vermeil with diamanté rhinestones and
pink, faceted, custom-shaped glass stone. $168.00

Brown seahorse with golden eye. $48.00

Reinad gold-plated marlin with diamanté accents. $285.00

Esteé Lauder fish opens to solid perfume, (White Linen), 1992. $100.00

Trifari sailfish. $125.00

Well-dressed lobster. $92.00

JJ fish.
Seed pearl and blue enamel. $30.00
Same fish in enamel $38.00

Red plastic sailfish. $92.00

ART seashell parure: necklace, bracelet, and earrings. $82.00

Persian jointed-fish necklace
complete with bells. $45.00

Sea lion sweethearts. $54.00

Walrus with faux-ivory tusks. $48.00

JJ dolphin. $40.00

BSK enamel seahorse. $50.00

Alvaire sterling silver fish. $94.00

Ciner pink fish. $85.00

Cadaro red and green cabochon fish. $450.00

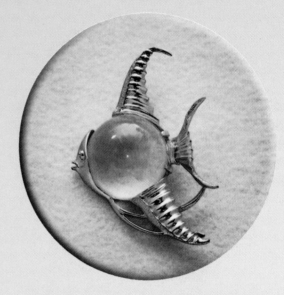

Cathe Lucite jelly-belly angel fish. $185.00

Ann Chez starfish earrings. $30.00

Ciner seahorse. $85.00

Mamcelle Originals by Ballet
clam shell pin is filled with golden grains
of sand and pearls. $85.00

Jewelarama seahorse with
mother-of-pearl ball. $58.00

De Nicola pearl-encrusted lobster. $145.00

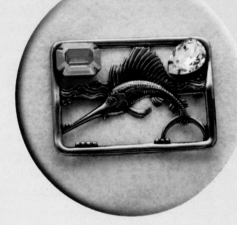

Sadie Green sailfish. $210.00

"E" Elizabeth Taylor.
Pisces fish and earrings.
Note pearl bubbles. $295.00

Thelma Deutsch blue seahorse. $98.00
Dalsheim starfish. $44.00

De Nicola fish with pearl. $114.00

SAC bracelet with charms from under the sea, 1950s. $48.00

Gold-plated sea horse with blue rhinestones. $22.00

Gold-tone seahorse with pavé head, red rhinestone eye, and green enamel body. $22.00

Sterling silver seahorse with matching earrings. $85.00

Silver shrimp has pavé head and tail with blue glass body. $28.00

Gold shrimp with faux pearls, pavé accents, and pink plastic shell. $55.00

Fish scatter pins. $20.00 (pair)

Sterling silver fish and earrings. $88.00

Blue rhinestone crab. $12.00

Lucite jelly-belly crab. $55.00

1930s pavé-finned fish with Burma
red rhinestone body. $195.00

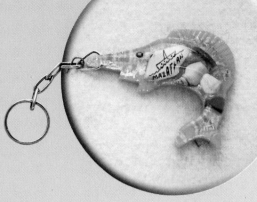

"Mazatlan" seashell fish. $18.00

Ann Klein seahorse. $25.00

Ann Klein starfish. $25.00

Sterling silver, reverse-carved,
Lucite jelly-belly fish. $225.00

This fish has a green enamel body and
hand-painted fins and tail. $45.00

Multicolored, silverplated fish. $55.00

1930s hand-set multicolored
rhinestone fish. $78.00

Now this is really a gold fish! $48.00

Pink baguettes encrust the body of this 1930s,
pavé-framed blowfish. $95.00

Gold-plated fish. $42.00

Red-scaled glass body is repeated
on matching earrings. $115.00

Cream enamel fish enlivened
by rhinestone scales. $35.00

Scatter pins with blue and
red glass bellies. $88.00 (pair)

Blue-finned fish. $48.00

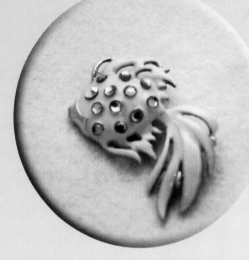

Cream-colored enamel fish accented
with pink rhinestone cabochons. $48.00

Black goldfish. $18.00

Gold-plated carp with
white enameling. $55.00

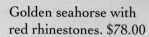

Golden seahorse with
red rhinestones. $78.00

Silver fish earrings have
faux pearls. $45.00

HAR pieces.
Novelty fish has red
and black belly glass. $38.00
Enamel fish has green rosette scales. $58.00

Esteé Lauder fish with solid perfume. $38.00

Trifari pavé fish with green enamel face,
fins, and tail. $150.00
Coro sword fish has jelly-belly and red
rhinestone top fin. $650.00

CoroCraft large-mouth fish.
Sterling fur clips with blue glass. $160.00
Stunning brooch with colorful fins, pavé
accents, and large, blue glass stone. $495.00

TRIP TO THE ZOO

Teddy bear with hand-painted
belly. $35.00

Tara animals all around the world,
gold-plated finish. $48.00

JJ bear climbing on a tree swing. $35.00

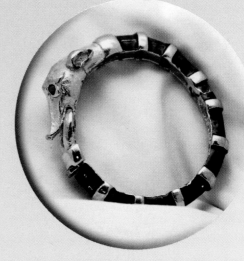

KJL bracelet, clasp locks directly
in mouth. $110.00

Castlecliff gazelle. $65.00
KJL dinosaur. $135.00
Monet teddy bear $65.00

JJ "Wiley Coyote" meets a cactus. $30.00

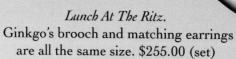

Lunch At The Ritz.
Ginkgo's brooch and matching earrings
are all the same size. $255.00 (set)

Happy hippo. $55.00

Capri hedgehogs. $34.00 (each)

Vendome menagerie with faux-turquoise
and green rhinestone accents.
Tiger. $145.00
Griffin. $145.00
Elephant with mahout. $175.00

Jomaz crocodile with green enamel. $125.00
Hattie Carnegie gazelle with plastic coral and
turquoise . $145.00

KJL white leopard with colorful cabochons.
Made in China. $110.00
KJL for Avon elephant necklace with enamel
accents on head and blanket. $54.00
KJL spotted leopard with pavé accents. $68.00

Napier elephant. $30.00
ART "king of the jungle." $70.00
ART ostrich, head is down. $48.00

Hobé critters.
Banana-eating monkey with pearl accents. $60.00
Smiling alligator with faux-coral accents. $50.00
Leaping leopard with rhinestone eyes. $140.00

Kenneth Lane enamel, spotted leopard
with pavé ribbon. $74.00
Jomaz giraffe with pavé ear. $140.00
Jomaz lion with pavé whiskers. $125.00

Trifari green cabochon crocodile. $95.00

Alligator hut earrings. $18.00

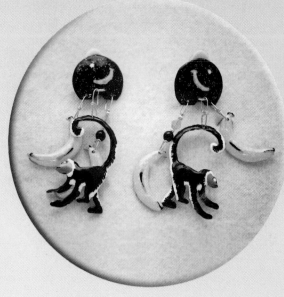

Lunch At The Ritz swinging monkeys. $65.00

Two-by-two giraffe brooch. $35.00
Blue rhinestone giraffe pin. $75.00

JJ giraffe. $38.00

White enamel giraffe. $48.00
Yellow and black enamel giraffe. $35.00

Trifari giraffe. $165.00

1930s rhinestone giraffe,
pink and red. $110.00

Willie Woo 1930s yellow giraffe with
red rhinestone spots. $105.00

Silver giraffe. $45.00

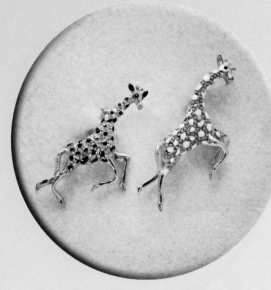

Black and diamanté giraffe. $65.00
Turquoise and milkstone giraffe. $58.00

Golden ostrich. $48.00
1930s rhinestone ostrich. $65.00

JJ zebra. $48.00

Trifari two-headed zebra brooch. $150.00

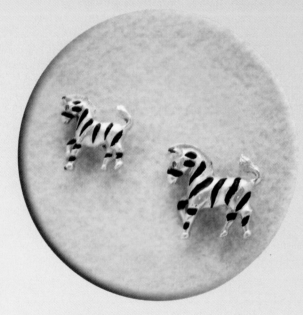

Pair of silver zebras. $35.00

Trifari zebra. $95.00

Silver zebra. $25.00

Zebra's stripes are interlaced with gold. $55.00

Wendy Gill running giraffe trembler. $210.00

Running zebra. $48.00

Shoulder-riding zebra. $68.00

Mylu reindeer trimmed with holiday ornaments. $110.00

Jeanne reindeer has green and red ornaments. $130.00

LIA reindeer with saddle and toys. $44.00

Graceful gazelle with dark green rhinestones. $25.00

Rhinestone gazelle. $38.00

Wooden-disc necklace features giraffe and zebra characters. Matching earrings not shown. $68.00

Close-up shows animal details.

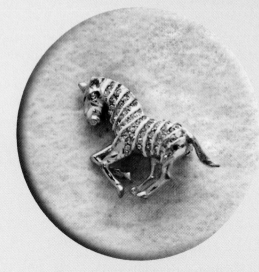

Hattie Carneige zebra. $195.00

Silver panda bear. $65.00

Burmese panda bear. $125.00

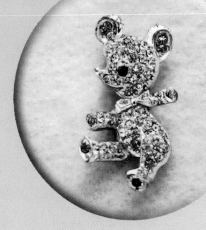

Pell teddy bear. $30.00

De Nicola ram's-head brooch. $95.00

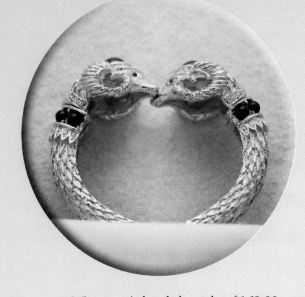

Cadaro ram's-heads bracelet. $168.00

KJL for Avon ram's-heads bracelet. $80.00

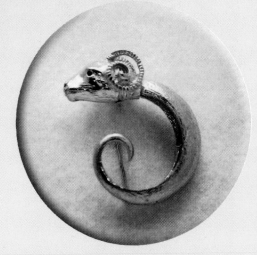

Jeanne ram's-head brooch. $48.00

Hattie Carnegie rams.
Ram's head ring with white plastic head. $125.00
Ram's head earrings with blue plastic head.
$200.00

KJL for Avon ram's head parure.
Double-strand necklace, brooch,
and earrings. $350.00

Joseff elephant necklace and earrings. $625.00

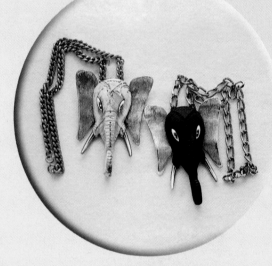

Razza necklaces.
Resin elephant with gold ears and tusks. $95.00
Black elephant with silver ears and tusks. $85.00

Enamel ibex. $38.00
Enamel ram's head, 1930s. $85.00
Ostrich with buried head. $60.00

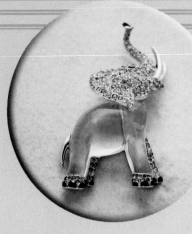

Trifari jelly-belly elephant fur clip with pavé head and feet. $1,700.00

Trifari red-bellied elephant with tear-drop cabochons. $110.00
Hollycraft enamel monkey complete with belly button. $85.00

Swarovski elephant. $75.00

Warner diamanté elephant with baguette blanket. $105.00

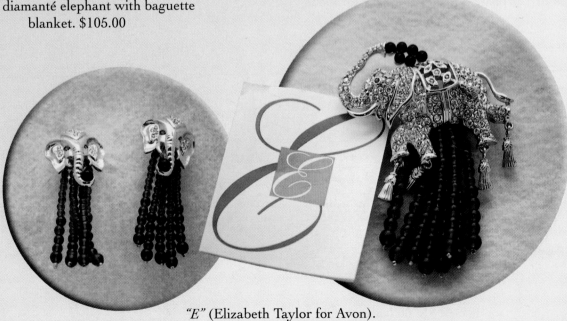

"E" (Elizabeth Taylor for Avon). Elephant brooch with earrings. $350.00

Elephant necklace with pearl drop. $40.00

JJ elephant with golden tusks. $34.00

Swinging elephant with articulated head. $48.00

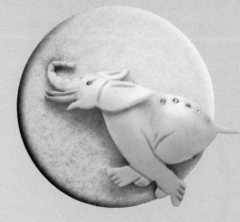

French (faux) ivory elephant. $250.00

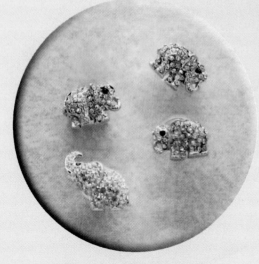

Elephant tie tacs. $15.00 (each)
Elephant earrings. $25.00

Trifari baby elephants. $80.00 (each)
Original by Robert seal balances ball. $95.00

Tortolani elephants.
Pill box. $145.00
Brooch. $95.00

KJL faux-ivory tusk necklace with elephant. $128.00
KJL pavé lion has turquoise eyes. $145.00
Lisner lion has bright red nose. $42.00

Close-up of necklace.

Trio of carved elephants on red bead
necklace with silver accents. $88.00

Pavé elephant bracelet. $44.00

Alana Stewart
zebra with turquoise eyes and mane.
Comes with matching earrings. $110.00

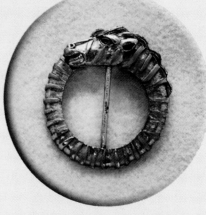

Zebra scarf holder. $28.00

211

CAT HOUSE

Joseff grand lion parure.
Necklace, brooch, bracelet,
and earrings. $1,200.00

KJL tiger bracelet. $85.00

Joseff of Hollywood lion brooch with large,
pear-shaped drop and five chains. $650.00

KJL for Avon leopard
necklace and earrings. $145.00

Close-up of
pendant detail.

Bead necklace with inlaid tiger pendant.
Comes with matching earrings (not shown). $275.00

Trifari big cats.
Lion has pavé on mane and tip of tail. $188.00
Stripped tiger has garnet rhinestone eyes.
$125.00

Creeping lion. $42.00
Murano glass tiger necklace. $58.00

Unusual lion has rattail mane surrounding
his heart-shaped rhinestone face. $185.00

Mazer lion has pavé whiskers and a
friendly expression. $128.00
Romantic lion carries a bouquet of
rhinestone flowers. $34.00

Leopard shows his spots. $48.00

Black plastic leopard, diamanté studded. $68.00

Roaring lioness. $65.00

Playful tiger with enlarged head. $83.00

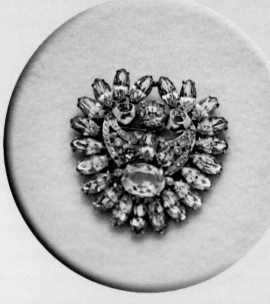

Plastic lion behind
rhinestone bush. $55.00

Diamanté lion head with full mane. $58.00

Lazy leopard. $42.00

Lion statue. $24.00

Lion magnifying glass. $40.00

Shoulder-riding lion. $85.00

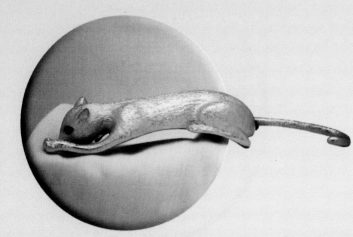

Shoulder-hugger lion. $48.00

Shoulder-riding leopard. $65.00

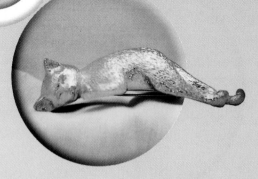

Shoulder-hugger lion. $45.00

Gerry enamel lion. $20.00

JJ golden lion. $30.00

Artifacts by JJ silver leopard
peeking through grass. $38.00

Gerry Lion's Club pin. $54.00

Gerry enamel lions. $18.00 (each)

Pavé leopard parure.
Necklace, bracelet, and earrings. $110.00

Roaring tiger. $75.00

Trifari "Safari" lazy leopard. $165.00

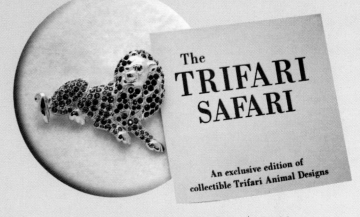

Trifari "Safari" rhinestone lion. $175.00

Tiger head with matching earrings. $110.00

Pavé leopard parure.
Bracelet fastens at head and tail, brooch
curves over shoulder, and earrings
match both. $105.00

217

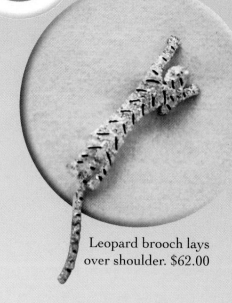

Leopard brooch lays
over shoulder. $62.00

A. Faberge lion necklace. $72.00
Emmons bob cat. $65.00

Giovanni lion. $36.00

Pavé leopard. $75.00

De Nicola fanciful lion. $110.00

Arthur M. Ross Co. Inc. japanned, dimensional,
pink cat with peridot navette eyes. $98.00

Leopard bracelet wrap. $38.00

Vogue lion with pavé saddle blanket. $80.00

Park Lane cheetah. $65.00

Mandle lion has gold chain top knot. $98.00
Joseph Mazer tiger has pavé nose and black stripes. $125.00

Nataly roaring tiger with black
enamel stripes. $84.00

Park Lane majestic lion necklace. $68.00

Castlecliff lion cuff bracelet. $250.00

Jewelarama lion with full mane. $38.00
Tiger with green rhinestone eye and pavé stripes. $78.00

Razza necklaces.
Resin lion with full mane. $85.00
Black ram with silver horns. $85.00

Les Bernard sterling golden lion. $75.00
Eisenberg Ice striped elephant. $68.00

Kenneth Lane lion door knocker. $105.00

Accessorcraft N.Y.C. dress belt with
lion's-head clasp, 1950s. $65.00

CIRCUS, CIRCUS

AJC circus tent has performers getting ready for the show. $45.00

Hobé clown has red, white, and blue beads. $225.00

Lisner clown face, pink cabochon with pavé nose. $65.00

Singing clown. $42.00
Clown's balloons. $15.00

Reja clown fur clip and earrings. $275.00

KJL pink elephant. $135.00
KJL coral-eyed monkey. $195.00
Pavé elephant. $78.00

R. *Mandel* cornelian cabochon circus horse. $135.00

Trifari elephants.
White enamel with blue accents. $155.00
Golden elephant with crown. $130.00

Carousel horse, gold plated. $30.00

Vogue Sterling "Leo" has red
rhinestone crown. $65.00

Silver elephant with blue rhinestones. $28.00
Enamel elephant with faux-ivory tusks. $75.00

Ornate elephant. $85.00

Florenza dancing poodle. $45.00

Pavé elephant doing his trick. $78.00

Gold elephant offers flowers. $22.00
Silver elephant dances. $35.00

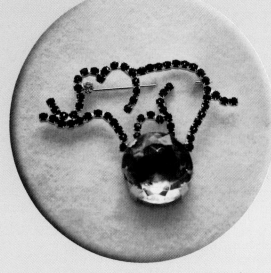

Rhinestone elephant balances on ball. $85.00

JJ royal elephant. $48.00

Elephant riding his scooter. $95.00

Monkey on tricycle. $28.00
Dancing bear. $55.00

Gray enamel elephants with their
malhouts. $50.00 (pair)
Black elephant with malhout in red
and blue. $85.00

Organ grinder's monkey $48.00

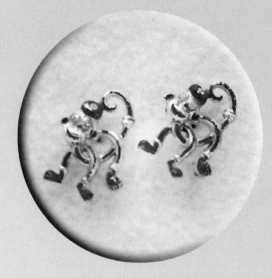

Dancing monkeys. $25.00 (pair)

Schaprelli circus line brooch. $495.00

JJ magic rabbit. $30.00

Elephant with trunk nosegay. $38.00

Gerry grey enamel monkey. $18.00
Jeanne dancing dog balances a flowerpot. $52.00

Florenza plumed, dancing horse. $110.00

Prancing, plumed, enamel horse
has rhinestone halter. $95.00

HAR animals.
Dancing enamel dog with hat and pipe. $54.00
Enamel monkey with hat and vest. $65.00

Clown is ready to charm the crowd. $38.00

Coro carousel. $195.00

Tortolani figurals.
Dancing clown comes in enamel and gold-plate.
Rocking clown comes in silver and enamel. $85.00 (each)

KJL elephants.
Elephant in tutu. $95.00
Elephant with turquoise accents. $180.00

Hattie Carnegie pins.
Plastic clown head. $110.00
Oriental soothsayer/medicine man. $235.00

Jomaz elephant with
colorful headdress. $245.00

Laughing clown. $125.00

Clown with flexible legs and arms. $35.00

Golden clown. $45.00
Jointed clown. $22.00

JJ snake charmer. $65.00

1990s articulated clowns. $18.00 (each)

Circus elephant with bell. $85.00

Whimsicals

BASKETS

Pearlized vase with red flowers. $18.00
Greenwich pink basket. $25.00

Coro diamanté basket with bow on top. $105.00
ART white enamel basket and leaves, edged in gold,
has blue navette rhinestones. $62.00
Monet vase fur clip will hold fresh flowers,
sterling. $95.00

Trifari, diamanté flowers. $65.00
Weiss sterling basket. $54.00

Trifari enamel basket with roses and daffodils. $54.00
Coro basket has purple stone cabochons. $85.00

Lawrence Vrba, pink faceted glass stones.
Designer has incorporated pearls, rhinestones,
and gold leaves. Earrings follow the pattern. $350.00

Ribbed basket contains stalks of red
rhinestone flowers. $42.00

Mazer pieces.
Pink moonstones accent this vase
pin and earring set. $105.00
Glass stone flowers in shades of blue fill
this lovely diamanté basket. $425.00

Wiesner amethyst and pavé brooch with
matching drop earrings. $78.00

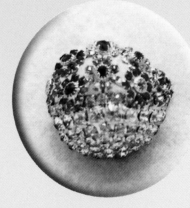

Bauer spring flower bouquet. $65.00

Suzanne Bjontegard, "Made in England." $110.00

Suzanne Bjontegard urn. $110.00

229

Bauer purple flower basket. $125.00

BSK Liza's flower basket from Lerner & Loewe's *My Fair Lady*. $55.00

Art Deco pin with rhinestone blooms. $95.00

Hand-set topaz petals encircle bouquet of citrine chaton rhinestones. $95.00

1930s metalwork basket. $275.00

1930s red rhinestone basket. $195.00

Purple rhinestone flowers fill silver basket. $55.00

Silver ribbed basket holds tiny rhinestone blooms. $65.00

White enamel basket holds stickpin flowers. $65.00

Enamel fruit basket. $48.00

Sweeping floral branches fall from basket. $125.00

Cornucopia brooch and earrings. $54.00

Display of metal craft. $75.00

Enamel flowers fill this basket with rhinetone accents. $75.00

Gold-plated basket shows off teal rhinestones bouquet. $35.00

Faux-turquoise basket and flowers. $65.00

Golden compote overflows with rhinestone blossoms. $35.00

Silverplated basket, handles form circle. $65.00

Long-stem blossoms in
wire basket. $30.00

Ribbed basket with colorful
bouquet. $80.00

Flower cart. $24.00
Tiny vase. $18.00

Nolan Miller floral basket. $110.00

ART blue enamel basket with
fuschia floral display. $52.00

Formal urn in muted
colors. $55.00

233

Basket and earrings. $25.00

Small rhinestone basket. $18.00

Lacy flowers fill this wicker
basket. $30.00

Basket of color. $55.00

Silverplated basket holds bouquet
with metal leaves. $48.00

Tiny pink flowers have aurora
borealis centers. $58.00

Silver basket with blue leaves and purple flowers. $35.00
Gold basket with gold and pink enamel hearts. $48.00

1930s floral arrangement. $110.00

Cornucopia with topaz flowers. $195.00

Gold wire basket with purple cabochons and blue flowers. $68.00
Diamanté basket filled with purple cabochons and lavendar ribbon. $75.00

Moonstone basket bouquets.
Purple. $64.00
White. $68.00

White Art Deco vase. $75.00

235

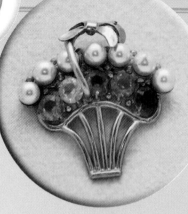

Row of pearls caps row of
chaton rhinestones. $68.00

1930s display of metal craft,
floral curls and basket. $145.00

Carved-glass tulips in flower cart. $95.00

Silver baskets filled with colorful blooms.
Navettes. $38.00
Cabochons and rhinestones. $42.00

Gold and silver leaves fill this lattice-
pattern basket. $25.00
Three "apple juice" Bakelite stones accent
basket of flowers. $125.00

Aurora borealis container with blooms
of fall color. $55.00
Frosted navettes complement the colors
of citrine basket. $18.00

Curved basket with spring mix. $65.00
Tiny basket with cabochons and rhinestones. $48.00

Pavé flower cart has three rhinestone flowers. $48.00
Watering can has large, purple stone. $21.00

Trio of tiny bouquets.
Pink daisies. $8.00
White roses. $42.00
Red geraniums. $28.00

Rhinestone-edged vase has classic,
sculptured lines. $75.00

1930s bezel-set rhinestones. $105.00

Silver basket with brilliant
blue flower. $65.00

Leo Glass formal design. $68.00

Basket of flowers in three shades of
green rhinestones and glass. $110.00

BSK flower cart from Lerner
& Loewe's *My Fair Lady*.
$70.00

Suzanne Bjontegard oval basket
with purple bow. $65.00

Miniature silver basket. $18.00
Silver basket with cabochons. $28.00
Gold open-weave basket. $35.00

Bouquets in miniature.
Basket is dotted with tiny pearls. $12.00
Silver, diamond weave basket is filled with pastel moonstones. $38.00
Tiny basket has single row of blue rhinestones in vase. $25.00
Gold, open-weave basket is filled with rhinestone-centered flowers. $45.00

ROYAL TREASURES

Ciner sword with coral handle. $185.00

Jolle Sterling sword with blue glass stones. $98.00

Blythe & Blythe red and gold baguette crown filled with teardrop rhinestones. $72.00

Nettie Rosenstein sterling.
Shield of armor with swords
and plumed helmet. $325.00
Ascot/stock sword pin. $275.00
Sword-hilt earrings. $94.00

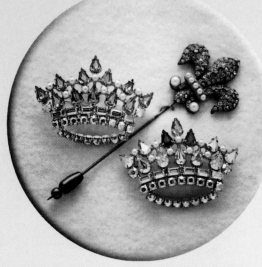

B. David crown in pink. $78.00
B. David crown in aurora borealis. $82.00
De Nicola hat pin fleur de lis. $110.00

Crowns chatelaine with opaline stones. $55.00

ART pearl-encrusted crown. $45.00

Dagger and sheath chatelaine with faux ruby and turquoise stones. $90.00

Silver-tone crown has three large glass stones and several small rhinestone accents. $110.00
Gold-tone crown has two large ruby cabochons, diamanté trim, and single row of rhinestones. $95.00

Cutlass and Turkish crown chatelaine with teal crystals. $85.00

Silver crown has a pavé sword attached by a chain. $18.00

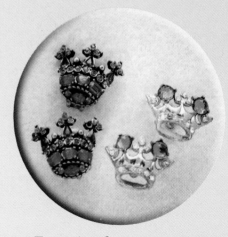

Two pairs of crown earrings.
Pink and peridot rhinestones. $35.00
Diamanté and blue rhinestones. $18.00

Crown scatter pins.
Opaline teardrop, pearl outline and
multi-colored rhinestones. $35.00 (pair)

Pell crown has pavé and pastel baguettes and
navette rhinestones. $125.00
Norris sterling crown has two large cabochons.
$195.00

Kramer crowns.
Five large chatons. $165.00
Seven diamanté navettes. $142.00

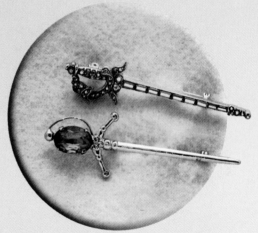

Pell sword has aurora borealis handle
and blue baguette blade. $85.00
Mizpah sword has topaz-faceted stone. $58.00

Kramer crowns.
Royal scepter has dangling crown charm. $185.00
Blue cabochon crown is surrounded by red
rhinestones. $84.00

Joseph Weisner cutlass.
Blue rhinestones. $98.00

Rhinestone crown with turquoise beads. $44.00
Sterling crown with sapphire cabochons. $58.00

Three-section crown. $48.00
English crown. $65.00

Royal key has two cabochons,
rhinestones, and pearls.
$55.00

Trifari pieces.
Key has faux sapphires and pearls. $110.00
Crown has faux pearls, carnelian, and jade. $145.00

Trifari pieces.
Crown has assortment of beautiful faux gems. $245.00
Sword has chain and removable tip. $210.00

Trifari royal emblems.
Tiny crown. $35.00
Scepter with large, pear-shaped diamanté stone. $98.00
Fleur de leis with faux ruby and emerald rhinestones. $88.00
Antique-gold fur clip with crown on top. $180.00

Trifari pavé and diamanté sword. $42.00
Weiss faux sapphire, ruby, and pearl crown.
$325.00

Trifari parure.
Sword, crown, and earrings. $550.00

Coro sword chatelaine can be worn as two brooches. $185.00
CoroCraft sword chatelaine can be sheathed. $245.00

De Rosa pearl and rhinestone crown, sterling.
$425.00
HAR pearl-topped royal staff. $115.00

CoroCraft collection.
Diamanté crown with sapphire
rhinestone accents. $165.00
Sterling vermeil crown and earrings
with faux gems. $195.00 (set)
Sterling crown with three large,
faceted rhinestones. $195.00

CoroCraft battle axe and helmet in polished-gold finish. $225.00
Trifari battle axe in beautiful shades of blue and gold. $225.00
Coro pavé key with faux sapphire and ruby accents. $185.00

Regency crown with topaz, gold, and champagne
rhinestones. $115.00
Castlecliff crown with red and diamanté
rhinestones, and three pearls on crown peak. $225.00

KJL medieval sconce. $165.00

KJL for Avon crown sparkles with
brilliant accents. $48.00
Jomaz crown has beautiful faux-
gem tassels. $195.00

Diamanté cutlass. $40.00
HAR crown. $58.00
Ornate sword brooch. $45.00

Pennino royal crown with red and
diamanté rhinestones. $180.00
ART Trojan helmet in stunning
royal colors. $68.00

Mosell NY full suit of armor.
Jointed arms and legs give
full range of motion. $1,800.00

Parisian Lights by Vonelle checkerboard
necklace. $54.00

Trifari chess pieces.
King and queen brooches, bright fur clips in black and white, and rook earrings. $650.00 (set)

Necklace has an assortment of charms including daggers and chess pieces. $74.00

THINGS WE USE

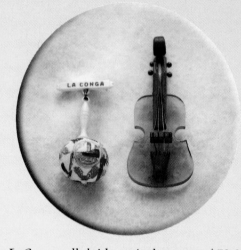

LaConga celluloid musical maraca. $38.00
Lucite and carved-wood bass guitar. $98.00

Dominique red, white, and blue rhinestone drum. $68.00

JJ saxophone. $35.00

Jolle banjo with pink crystal glass. $79.00

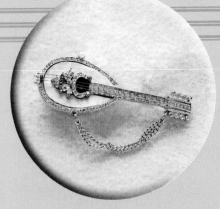

Gene Verracchi by Gem-Craft mandolin paid homage to R. Mandel and his beautiful jewelry designs. $45.00

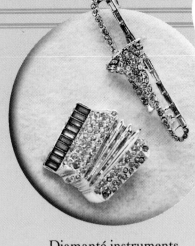

Diamanté instruments.
Accordion. $38.00
Trombone. $24.00

Treble clef. $18.00
Musical chord. $54.00
Quarter note. $12.00

Mandolin has ruby accents. $95.00

Classical lyre. $35.00
Golden harp. $24.00

Tiny violin. $8.00
Onyx and turquoise mandolin. $95.00
Silver guitar. $22.00

Bugle and drums (red, white, and blue). $55.00

Juliana green rhinestone violin. $85.00

Weisner pavé guitar with rich
blue rhinestones. $68.00

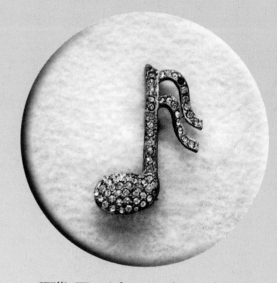

Willie Woo pink musical note. $28.00

Tara cello with rhinestone accents. $48.00

Coro Philharmonic series lyre, sterling. $170.00
Original by Robert aurora borealis cello. $155.00

Joseff bell parure. Necklace, bracelet, and earrings. $750.00

1940s two-part scatter pin telephone. $35.00
1930s silver phone. $18.00

Gold telephone, rhinestone studded. $28.00

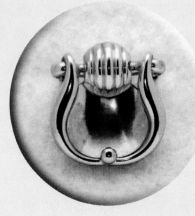

Grosse Germany door knocker, 1977. $125.00

Battery-operated ringing telephone. $25.00

Renoir/Matisse artist's palette, copper brooch. $75.00

California Art lucite barrel-with-bow brooch becomes a watch when you look at the bottom. $98.00

UR Creations key to worlds unknown, maybe even to a heart. $74.00

Kirks Folly scales of Libra. $54.00

BSK victrola. From Lerner & Loewe's *My Fair Lady.* $55.00

JJ school teacher's desk. $32.00

Fancy fish hook. $22.00
Bowling ball and pin. $18.00

Golf bag with three clubs. $22.00
Diamanté and black rhinestone clubs. $35.00

Sterling by Lang lantern with
red rhinestone flame. $68.00

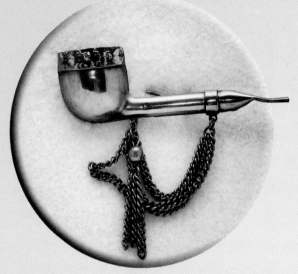

1940s gold-plated pipe with decorative triple chain. $68.00

Silver teapot. $10.00
Copper tea service. $35.00

Decorative fork and spoon. $12.00 (each)

Rhinestone hanger. $14.00
Rhinestone safety pin. $12.00

Rhinestone saw has two pieces,
a pin pushes into blade to fasten. $48.00
Pot-belly stove. $28.00

Rhinestone eye glasses. $18.00
Green striped bottle of bubbly fills
champagne glass. $38.00

AJC grapes, wine, and glasses. $18.00

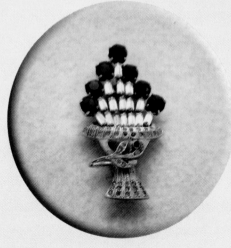

A fountain of clear baguettes topped with
blue sapphire rhinestones. $38.00

Aladdin's lamp sparkles in pavé and clear baguettes. $18.00
Rhinestone-studded dancing slipper. $18.00

Hollycraft postal lantern with red
bow and holly leaves. $85.00

Nemo claw-foot tub with golden bear. $32.00
Weiss lantern with red enamel roof,
novelty glass creates illusion of flame. $110.00

Coro pieces.
Door knocker with rhinestone accents. $98.00
Bejeweled lamp with decorative chain and
tassel. $185.00

Weiss rhinestone palette and paint brush. $175.00
Ora diamanté musical note. $38.00

Coro pieces.
Cuckoo clock with
pendulum and two chains. $195.00
Lion door knocker. $65.00
Faux-turquoise and floral garland
door knocker. $92.00

253

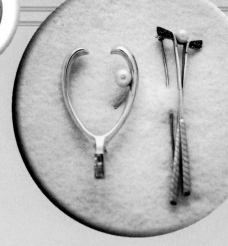

Trifari pieces with pearl accents.
Silver wishbone. $45.00
Golf clubs. $48.00

Original by Robert enamel pot-belly stove with
gold trim. $88.00
CoroCraft parasol with diamanté and red rhinestones. $145.00

Enco charm bracelet with hour glass. $35.00
Jomaz umbrella with bucket of pearl bubbles. $135.00

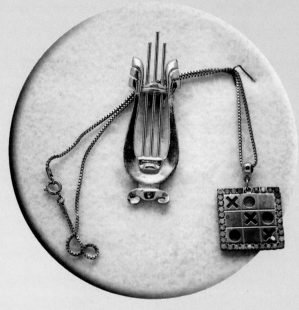

Monet lyre fur clip. $34.00
Hobé tic-tac-toe necklace. $45.00

Danecraft artist's pallet with charm dangles. $34.00
Canadian curling stone with diamanté accents. $24.00

Lawrence Vrba unfurled flag. $225.00

Antique ice skate. $18.00
Gold-tone scales. $30.00
Hollycraft street lamp necklace. $85.00

Bettina Von Walhof flag. $88.00

Czechoslovakia cuckoo clock. $45.00
Diamanté typewriter. $28.00
Castlecliff sterling clock. $58.00

Chanel flag. $475.00

Labou Mexico sterling jacket
has a swinging skirt. $74.00

Trifari fan with earrings. $68.00
Weiss flag. $45.00

W. Germany purse mirror. $12.00

Pair of dancing slippers. $25.00

Top hats and canes.
Red and blue rhinestones. $18.00
Red rhinestones on silver. $35.00

Three umbrellas for April showers.
Yellow. $35.00
Pink. $38.00
Green. $25.00

KJL enamel dress shoe with pink ribbon. $35.00

Jeanne high-top shoe with nosegay. $44.00

BSK two hats from Liza's
My Fair Lady wardrobe. $65.00

BSK, more wardrobe hats.
Professor's top hat and cane. $65.00
Liza's fashionable hat. $60.00

Top hat and cane brooches.
Small brooch has brilliant blue baguettes. $35.00
Large brooch has bright diamanté stones. $28.00

Tinted glasses have stems that open. $18.00

Thimble full of stick pins. $48.00
Scissors with blue stone accent. $12.00

BSK Liza's parasols in delicate enamel.
Comes opened or closed. $55.00 (each)

Gold-plated scissors. $35.00

Mexico Sterling place setting with fish. $58.00

Swiss by Picard sterling silver Alpine chalet. $92.00

Revolver and holster chatelaine
can become one brooch. $68.00

Sword in scabbard. $28.00
1920s old-fashioned parasol. $35.00

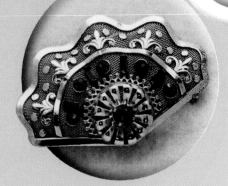

Bond Boyd sterling.
What lady wouldn't love this fan with
beautiful amethyst baguettes? $98.00

MYTHICAL BEASTS

Tortolani zodiac ram's-head ring, two views. $48.00
Hattie Carnegie "conscience" earrings:
devil and angel. $65.00 (pair)

Disney by Napier.
Gold-plated Mickey Mouse. $78.00

Trifari dragon necklace in
teal blue enamel. $75.00

Mosell fire-breathing dragon in red
and green rhinestones. $1,800.00

259

Trifari pavé unicorn. $150.00

Trifari pieces.
Zodiac pins: Leo and Taurus. $35.00 (each)
Mother Goose pin. $145.00

H. Pomerantz & Co. of NY silver-plated dragon. $48.00
P.I.M. Sagittarius archer. $72.00

"Harvey" sterling silver jelly-belly with
cane and top hat. $275.00

11 W. 30th St. green rhinestone dragon. $64.00

Playboy bunny, sterling silver. $85.00

Polcini zodiac ram perched on rhinestone rock. Detailing includes ears, goatee, and curling horns. $68.00

Griffin guards my treasures. $95.00

Pavé full body dragon. $175.00

Pavé-winged Pegasus, 1950s. $48.00

Gold-plated Pegasus, 1950s, coral and turquoise plastic body. $55.00

Blue-bellied dragon. $68.00

261

East Indian filigree dragon. $48.00

Chinese dragon with matching earrings. $95.00

Carved Chinese dragon, blue rhinestones. $36.00

The regal Phoenix. $85.00

Diamanté Phoenix, 1930s. $110.00

Leo, the lion, above faux-lapus stone. $55.00

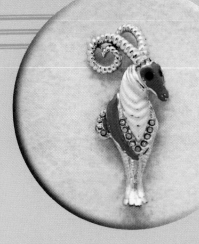

Molded plastic coral ram with turquoise body and head. $45.00

JJ Pegasus. $65.00

Butler & Wilson Chinese dragon. $165.00

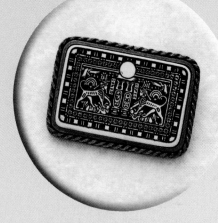

Chico's copy of ancient Egyptian temple guardians. $38.00

Capri flaming dragon protects pearl egg. $128.00

Korda dragon necklace. $185.00

Korda dragon brooch. $98.00

Korda Aladdin riding winged horse. $92.00

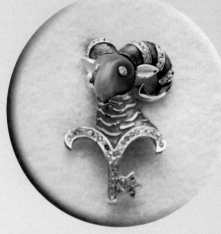

De Nicola Aries, the ram. $74.00

Sterling by Cini Taurus, the bull. $78.00

Edgar Berebi golden dragon with flame red rhinestones. $68.00

Dragon with a personality, green rhinestone belly. $35.00

HAR dragon grand parure.
Brooch, necklace, cuff bracelet, and earrings.
All have dragons and large glass novelty
stones. $1,800.00

Trifari dragon cuff bracelet, head and tail
are diamanté rhinestones. $165.00

Hattie Carnegie faux-coral dragon
necklace and drop earrings. $295.00

Hattie Carnegie beasts.
Fire-breathing dragon. $245.00
Fierce-looking lion. $260.00

Vendome unicorn with fuchsia and blue
rhinestones and turquoise beads. $125.00
KJL dragon with blue cabochon belly. $85.00
KJL Peking glass dragon with
scalloped pavé edges. $110.00

KJL dragon bracelet. $110.00

TRANSPORTATION

Sterling horse and buggy. $54.00
Copper-tone sailing ship. $28.00
Pink smoke-stack tug boat. $38.00

Hattie Carnegie Chinese junk. $255.00
Joseff Roman chariot. $350.00

Silson "Mercy Ship," made in Canada. $265.00

Tortolani "Hyde and Market Street" San
Francisco cable car. $125.00
Coro sterling sailing ship,
patent pending. $175.00

Pastel rhinestone locomotive
complete with cowcatcher. $48.00

Coro paddle-wheel boat in red, white,
and blue rhinestones. $255.00
Ora coach and driver with blue
baguette accents. $54.00

Hansom carriage with driver, sterling silver. Special touch shows the horse's hooves underneath the axle. $110.00

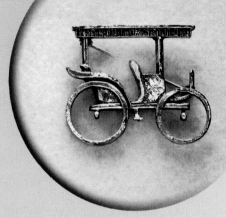

Zental surrey with a fringe on top. $55.00

Anchors away, (red, white, and blue) necklace. $65.00

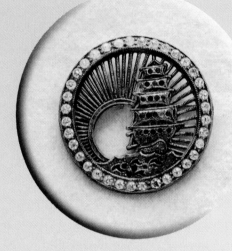

Ancient mast ship against the rays of the setting sun. $68.00

Oleg Cassini rickshaw. $95.00

Rickshaw with fan canopy. $38.00

Pavé wheelbarrow hauling diamonds. $35.00

Baby buggy, pavé with black accents. $47.00

Sterling silver coach, coachman,
and prancing horse. $110.00

Conestoga with oxen. $45.00

Lunch At The Ritz pieces.
Bracelet with steering wheel and tires. $185.00
Tie-tac ignition, complete with keys. $65.00

268   Spanish ship necklace with full sails
and mermaid on bow. $55.00

Bauer pavé airplane. $68.00

Plastic traffic signal.
Pull the color bead
and change signal arm from
green to red. $45.00

Old-fashioned steam engine. $38.00

San Francisco cable cars. $30.00 – 40.00 (each)

Sailboat on the ocean blue. $78.00
Submarine. $28.00
Venice canal gondola. $22.00

1940s flight of planes. $15.00 – 25.00 (each)

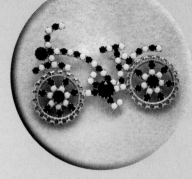

Black and white bicycle. $28.00

Red, white, and blue sailboat. $65.00

Sailboat of navettes. $40.00

Antique coach. $28.00

Sterling silver horse and cart. $78.00

Roadsters with rumble seats. $24.00 (each)

Touring car, 1930s. $24.00
"Checker" taxi cab. $18.00

1930s metal brooches with multi-color
rhinestone accents.
Paddle-wheel boat. $145.00
Conestoga wagon. $125.00
Western stagecoach. $168.00

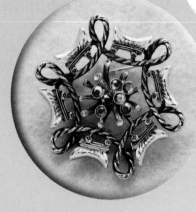

SAC covered wagons circle the campfire. $65.00

Venice canal gondola. $45.00
Spanish ship of old. $65.00

Kirks Folly Santa's sleigh. $245.00

Bauer red, white, and blue sailboat. $105.00

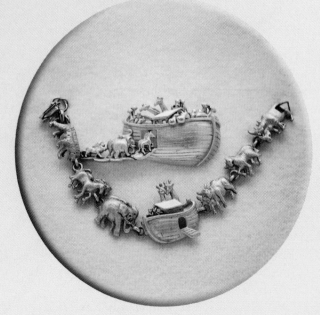

AJC Noah's Ark pieces.
Brooch. $30.00
Bracelet. $45.00

271

TUTTI-FRUTTI

Glass lemons adorn this colorful necklace. $85.00
Kramer pineapple with woven gold overlay. $48.00

Boucher pineapple. $75.00
Lisner pumpkin. $62.00

Coro artichoke in green enamel. $48.00
Francois apple in two shades of blue. $68.00

Hobé cherry. $65.00
Boucher red raspberry. $225.00

Vendome apple and pears,
both missing a bite. $150.00
Napier red apples on branch. $45.00
Napier brushed gold apple. $55.00

Austria berry brooch and earrings. $85.00 (set)
Hattie Carnegie sliced apple. $98.00

Austria orange brooch and earrings. $58.00 (set)
Eisenberg Original plum fur clip. $850.00

Eisenberg Ice strawberry with
fuchsia rhinestone. $55.00
HAR pineapple with faux-
turquoise beads. $30.00

Alice Caviness fruits.
Pearl-studded pineapple. $70.00
Rhinestone-studded pineapple. $55.00

Original by Robert enamel fruits.
Strawberry. $45.00
Red delicious apple. $60.00
Yellow delicious apple. $45.00

HAR D'Anjou pear. $60.00
Nettie Rosenstein apple fur clip. $165.00
HAR red apple. $54.00

Nettie Rosenstein bag with golden strawberry
brooch and earrings. $350.00

Weiss fruit brooch and earring sets.
Cherries. $145.00
Strawberries. $60.00

HAR fruits.
D'Anjou enamel pear. $60.00
Cherry brooches, enamel. $75.00 (each)

Weiss berries.
Silver rhinestone
strawberry brooch and earrings. $110.00
Red rhinestone strawberry scatter pins. $95.00 (pair)

Weiss red enamel apple. $48.00
Trifari white enamel strawberry
with matching earrings. $68.00

Kramer plum. $65.00

Hollycraft twin cherry brooches. $50.00 (each)

Kramer white enamel, red rhinestone
strawberry brooch and earrings. $74.00

Kramer satin-finish pear brooch
and earrings. $140.00

Pell red rhinestone strawberry and apple
with green baguette accents. $68.00
Miriam Haskell enamel apple. $48.00

W green strawberry. $45.00

Thailand red berries, two-tone
green leaves and stem. $68.00

Warner raspberry brooch and earrings with
japanned backing has red rhinestones, dark
green leaves, and black stems. $85.00

SAC golden delicious apple brooch
and earrings. $32.00

Austria red cherry pin and earrings. $65.00

Austria red apple pin and earrings. $60.00

Austria raspberries.
Silver leaves and blue raspberries.
Green leaves and red raspberries. $50.00 (each)

Austria blue pear pins and earrings. $65.00

Austria strawberry pin and earrings. $70.00

Austria orange pears. $55.00
Cream pear. $38.00

Austria gold rhinestone pear pin and
earrings in Lucite base. $42.00

Austria black rhinestone pear pin and
earrings in Lucite base. $48.00

Austria blue nectarberries and earrings
with purple blush. $55.00

Austria red delicious apples and earrings
have a blush of color. $58.00

Austria green apples with matching earrings
have a dark green blush. $65.00

Austria, special plums.
Purple. $52.00
Deep blue. $45.00

Austria apples.
Red. $32.00
Silver. $48.00

Austria leaf earrings. $24.00
Austria blueberry. $32.00

Austria blackberries with matching earrings. $68.00

Austria fruit brooches.
Green apples. $50.00
Lemons. $35.00

ART apple with matching earings. $85.00

ART rhinestone berry. $28.00

ART enamel pear. $48.00

ART orange blossom earrings. $38.00

279

SAC red berries. $22.00

Golden pineapple. $32.00

Red strawberry. $12.00

BSK black pear. $45.00

BSK golden pear and earrings,
satin finish. $75.00

1930s grape cluster. $68.00

Moonstone grape cluster
dress clip. $90.00

Pink rhinestone grape
cluster dress clip. $125.00

Strawberry pin and earrings. $48.00

Red plastic chain necklace with double row
of berries and leaves. $175.00

Stylized pear. $28.00

Enamel pear. $38.00
Rhinestone pear. $45.00

Fruit trees with enamel fruit and leaves
and single bird perched in branches.
Cherry. $24.00
Apple. $24.00

Moonstone grape cluster. $85.00

Small pineapple. $10.00
Red-cheeked pear. $28.00

Vine grapes
with leaf. $44.00

Clear apple with blue rhinestones. $45.00
Black apple with light blue stones. $32.00

Reverse-carved jelly-belly apple. $110.00

Rhinestone-studded fruit.
Blue pear. $38.00
Red strawberry. $48.00

Berry with seed pearls and red rhinestones. $24.00

Kenneth Jay Lane citrine and topaz
fruit with dark green rhinestone leaves. $95.00

WHIMSIES

Marine building 1939
New York World's Fair
(NYWF). $165.00

GA "Seattle's World's Fair, 1962"
space needle brooch and earrings. $98.00

Miriam Haskell feathers.
Real feather earrings with aurora
borealis stones. $225.00.
Lucite feather brooch with floral, pastel
beadwork. $475.00

Golden Gate International Exposition
(GGIE) building. $175.00

Arrow with heart chatelaine. $78.00
Miriam Haskell key. $110.00

Coro sterling heart has bird in center. $58.00
Trifari "Betty Crocker Homemakers
of Tomorrow" heart brooch. $65.00

Leru diamanté-trimmed red heart brooch
with matching earrings. $105.00

The wings of love guide Cupid's arrow. $82.00

1930s dark red glass stones form feathers
and spear head of this arrow. $140.00

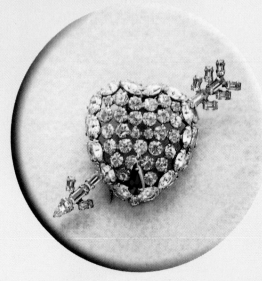

Benreig diamanté heart with red teardrop. $108.00

Valentine hearts, brooch with earrings. $88.00

Gene Verracchi pearl, aurora borealis, and cabochon heart. $45.00

Karu dog-toothed settings hold aurora borealis and purple rhinestones. Heart has matching earrings. $85.00

E (Elizabeth Taylor for Avon) has opaline stone center. $110.00

Austria heart in purple and pink rhinestones. $55.00

Love's arrow. $28.00

Kirks Folly heart-shaped earrings. $40.00

Chanel diamanté arrow. $550.00

Hollycraft triple-chain heart necklace.
Heart with dangling arrows is the
longest point. $110.00

Fashioncraft black heart framed by pearl-shaped
red stones and pearls. $225.00

Coro hearts.
Red and diamanté rhinestone
heart and earrings. $150.00
Heart has multicolored stones. $95.00

Coro lover's arrow brooch
and earrings with red rhinestones. $69.00
Napier black and diamanté heart necklace. $48.00

Jeanne four-leaf clover. $38.00

Trifari peas (pearls) in a golden pod. $180.00
Castlecliff peas (pearls) in a golden pod. $85.00

Lunch At The Ritz South Western earrings
complete with boots. $105.00

Weiss four-leaf clovers.
Gold rhinestone brooch. $45.00
Gold, slightly cupped petals with
matching earrings. $70.00

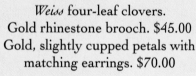

The holiday door opens
to the tree and children. $40.00

Bright red lollipop. $25.00

SAC family tree, decorated with rhinestones. $34.00

Kirks Folly man in the moon. $45.00

Reed & Barton sterling good-luck whistle necklace. $110.00

Beau Jewels convertible brooch has bug, frog, blue bird, and butterfly changes for the flower. $80.00

Cinerama Irish leprechaun's pot of gold. $28.00

Dominique wrapped green gift with
diamanté ribbon. $75.00

Hallmark 1982 brooch asks,
"Do you love me?" $35.00

Green as Ireland with shamrocks
and clay pipes. $42.00

Bauer sign speaks for itself. $90.00

Lunch At The Ritz
leprechaun's hat and all his charms. $250.00

Lunch At The Ritz frog prince.
Earring on left shows his crown.
Both hang from red hearts. $85.00

Wishing well with matching
flower earrings. $68.00

Question mark ends in
sapphire blue drop. $48.00

Love carvings on old tree trunk. $28.00

May all your wishes come true.

Sparkles

The wishing well was produced by *Staret*. Valued at $400.00

Glossary

Amethyst — natural gemstone in shades from lavender to purple. Costume jewelry frequently used imitation rhinestones in the same shades.

Antique — costume jewelry made before 1950.

Art Deco — style of geometric lines and bold colors, 1910-1930.

Articulated — divided into distinct segments that give the piece mobility.

Art Nouveau — designs centered on a poetic interpretation of nature, 1890-1915.

Aurora borealis — microscopic layers of different materials vacuum-plated to glass for iridescent coating.

Baguette — elongated, faceted, straight-sided stone.

Bakelite — phenolic plastic discovery of Leo H. Bakeland in 1909. Formula contains formaldehyde and carbolic acid.

Base metal — 92% tin with added cadmium, lead, and zinc. Used to form the first stage of a costume jewelry design. Can also be called pot metal or white metal.

Bezel — metal fitting completely surrounding the stone at the girdle. Each fitting is then shaped by a skilled artisan to tightly hold the stone in place.

Bling — computer slang for the word "fabulous".

Brooch — from the French *broche* which means skewer.

Burrs — small lumps of metal rising from the base metal and stationed around the stone to protect it from damage.

Cabochons — unfaceted, rounded, dome stones. Usually flat on underneath side.

Chatelaine — ornamental clasp worn at the waist with long chains from which hung all the items necessary for daily housekeeping. Now it is the name for two brooches connected by one or more chains.

Chaton — most common faceted rhinestone. A cut with 9 to 12 facets, flat table-top surface, bottom comes to a point.

Citrine — quartz stone ranging from yellow to gold in color. Imitated in rhinestones.

Collectibles — costume jewelry manufactured after 1950.

Contemporary — manufactured within the past twenty years.

Costume jewelry — jewelry not containing precious jewels or metals.

Diamanté — imitation diamonds. Another name for clear rhinestones.

Depossé — French term marked on the back of jewelry denoting patent pending in France.

Dogtoothed — setting with more prongs than the standard four. The multiple prongs surround the stone they are holding much like a dog's mouth when holding a ball.

Dress clip — hinged-clasp brooch, worn singularly or in pairs. Inserted on the neckline bunching the material together to create a lower neckline with ornamentation.

Earrings — pair of two matching ear ornaments. Counted as one.

Facets — cuts made to shape stones and enhance light refraction.

Faux — French for *false*. Used to denote man-made copies of gemstones.

Filigree — open, airy, lacy, decorative metal scroll work.

Flat-back — used to describe a stone that is flat and plain on the bottom. Can be either foiled or unfoiled.

Foil backing — backing applied to rhinestones in a vacuum-plating process using very thin gold or silver metal. This allows light to bounce off the stone and sparkle.

French ivory — imitation ivory. Cream-colored plastic with a grain copying the striations in elephant ivory. Very flammable.

Fur clip — two long prongs on a spring steel allow the decorative clip to be worn on heavy fabric or fur.

Grand parure — parure containing four matching pieces of jewelry.

Imitation diamond — clear rhinestones of such high quality they rival diamonds.

Japanned — a black, coal-tar derivative used as a finish coating.

Jelly-belly — name for figural brooches where Lucite (clear Plexiglass) stone is a major portion of the design.

Luicite — DuPont's trade name for Plexiglass, introduced during World War II.

Mabe pearl — cultured, abalone pearl.

Malachite — mineral of compact green variety with alternating irregular bands of light and dark green.

Marcasite — common crystallized iron pyrite.

Marquise — oval-shaped stone coming to a point on each end (resembling an eye), also called a navette.

Navette — stone, oval shaped with point on each end, also called marquise.

Opaline — man-made imitation of an opal.

Parure — more than two matching pieces of jewelry.

Patent Pending — a patent has been applied for, protecting the invention from use without the permission of the inventor. Usually pertains to a device. "Pat. Pend." is written on the back of jewelry.

Pavé — stones placed close together with a minimum of metal shown. Literally paving over the metal.

Pendant — ornamental drop that can be attached to necklace. Sometimes a pin will also be present to allow the pendant to be worn as a brooch.

Peridot — a light, rich green rhinestone imitating the gemstone.

Phenolics — cast and molded plastics of the 1920s. Bakelite is in this class.

Pill box — small container carried in purse or on bracelet to hold medications.

Plating — jewelry dipped in electro-magnetic, acid bath which forms a thin layer of finish.

Pot metal — see base metal.

Rat tail — woven chain used to imitate hair in costume jewelry designs.

Reintroduction — jewelry where the original master mold is brought out of company's archives for a new production run.

Reverse carving — carving worked from the underneath side.

Refraction — the deflection of a ray of light from a straight pattern.

Rhinestone — leaded-glass stone with foil backing.

Rosette — a group of closely-set gemstones arranged in a circular form around a center stone.

Scatter pins — a group of common theme small pins, usually two or three to a set. A style of the 1940s.

Shoulder hanger — brooch designed to drape over the shoulder of the wearer, can be seen from both back and front.

Shoulder-sitting — brooch designed to sit on the shoulder seam of the garment.

Set — more than one matching piece of same design.

Topaz — gemstone usually ranging in color from yellow to orange.

Vacuum plated — used in plating metal to glass. Several microscopic layers of different materials on the back of clear stock.

Vermeil — a gold wash over sterling silver. Can be pink or yellow gold finish.

White metal — see base metal.

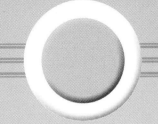

Bibliography

Ball, Joanne Dubbs. *Jewelry of the Stars*. West Chester, PA: Schiffer Publishing, Ltd., 1991.

Becker, Vivienne. *Rough Diamonds*. London, England: Pavilion Books, 1990.

Bell, Jeanenne. *How To Be A Jewelry Detective*. Shawnee, Kansas: A.D. Publishing, 2000.

Cera, Deanna Farretti. *The Jewels of Miriam Haskell*. Milan, Italy: Idea, 1997.

Dolan, Maryanne. *Collecting Rhinestone & Colored Jewelry*. Florence, AL: Books Americana, 1993.

Gerson, Roselyn. *The Esteé Lauder Solid Perfume Compact Collection 1967 to 2001*. Paducah, KY: Collector Books, 2002.

Lane, Kenneth Jay and Harrice Simons Miller. *Faking It*. New York, NY: Harry N. Abrams, Inc. 1996.

Leshner, Leigh. *Collecting Art Plastic Jewelry*. Iola, WI: KP Books, 2005.

Moro, Ginger. *European Designer Jewelry*. Atlen, PA: Schiffer Publishing Ltd., 1995.

Newman, Harold. *An Illustrated Dictionary of Jewelry*. New York, NY: Thames & Hudson, Inc., 1981.

Oshel, Kay. *Jewelry From Sarah Coventry and Emmons*. Atglen, PA: Schiffer Publishing Ltd., 2005.

Rainwater, Dorothy. *American Jewelry Manufacturers*. Atglen, PA: Schiffer Publishing Ltd., 1988.

Shatz, Sheryl Gross. *What's It Made Of?* Santa Ana, CA: Benjamin Shatz, 1992.

Simonds, Cherri. *Collectible Costume Jewelry*. Paducah, KY: Collector Books, 1997.

Vintage Fashion and Costume Jewelry Newsletter, Glen Oaks, NY.

White, Palmer. *Elsa Schiaparelli*. New York, NY: Rizzoli International Publications, Inc., 1980.

Index

About the Author

I am often asked where I got the middle name of "Sparkles." It all began when my husband took note of my attraction to rhinestone jewelry. He saw that a certain glow came over me when I looked at a shining item for sale. It wasn't long before he began to call out, "Sparkles, here is something you should see". And that was the birth of my middle name.

That beginning has taken me to many places. Venture Entertainment offered me the opportunity to host and co-write seven tapes for the "Hidden Treasures: A Collector's Guide to Antique and Vintage Jewelry" award winning series.

Drawing upon 12 years of experience as a free-lance newspaper correspondent for Oregon newspapers, my articles have been featured in *Vintage Fashion and Costume Jewelry* and in various antique newspapers.

As an active member of the Southern Oregon Antiques & Collectibles Club, I have served on its board for over ten years. My appraisal services have been used by the Grimes' Calendar Shows, the Palmer Whirf Shows, and Medford SOACC Shows. Since 1996, I have served as the rhinestone jewelry advisor and contributor for *Schroeder's Antique Price Guide*, and *Garage Sale & Flea Market Annual*.

As an antique and vintage jewelry historian, lecturer, and collector, I have enjoyed sharing my knowledge and jewelry with many dealers, mall owners, and collectors throughout the years.

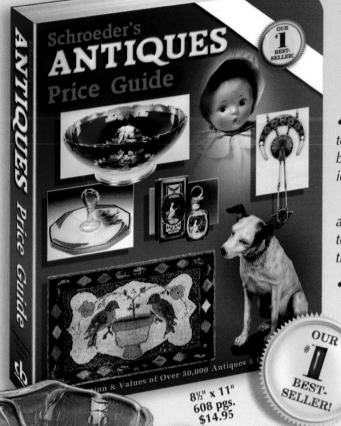